BILL SHIELL

The Door To A Joyful Life

LOSERSHIP

Smyth & Helwys Books
6316 Peake Road
Macon, Georgia 31210-3960
1-800-747-3016
©2025 by William D. (Bill) Shiell
All rights reserved.

Library of Congress Cataloging-in-Publication Data

Names: Shiell, WIlliam David, 1972- author.
Title: Losership : the door to a joyful life / by WIlliam D. Shiell.
Identifiers: LCCN 2025001747 | ISBN 9781641735872 (paperback)
Subjects: LCSH: Failure (Psychology)--Religious aspects--Christianity. |
Self-actualization (Psychology)--Religious aspects--Christianity.
Classification: LCC BT730.5 .S55 2025 | DDC 248.4--dc23/eng/20250328
LC record available at https://lccn.loc.gov/2025001747

Disclaimer of Liability: With respect to statements of opinion or fact available in this work of nonfiction, Smyth & Helwys Books, an imprint of Smyth & Helwys, LLC, nor any of its employees, makes any warranty, express or implied, or assumes any legal liability or responsibility for the accuracy or completeness of any information disclosed, or represents that its use would not infringe privately-owned rights.

Advance Praise for *Losership: The Door to a Joyful Life*

In this wise and instructive book, Bill Shiell has paired experiences from his own story with examples from the pages of scripture to give high school and college students practical tools to navigate "lifequakes" that inevitably will come their way not once but often as the years increase. A valuable resource for students and all who come alongside them in mentoring, teaching, or parental capacities.

—Jeff Crosby
author of *The Language of the Soul and World of Wonders: A Spirituality of Reading*

Fortunate are those who are told the truth about life and the challenges it presents. Even more fortunate are those who have a trusted guide who will love them, walk with them, and direct them to find God's presence in the most challenging circumstances. Bill Shiell is that trusted guide. This book is not only a manual for those who will experience difficulty but also for those who desire to emerge more faithful and resilient on the other side.

—Kyle Reese
Senior Minister, First Baptist Church
Savannah, Georgia

In *Losership*, Dr. Bill Shiell challenges our cultural obsession with achievement, reframing success through the lens of Jesus' upside-down kingdom. He shows how failure, loss, and setbacks can be redemptive moments that lead to God's joy and transformation. This is a must-read for anyone navigating change, uncertainty, or seeking deeper purpose.

— Rev. Nick Hughes
Senior Pastor, Mountain Chapel Methodist Church,
Birmingham, Alabama

From his own personal experience and keen biblical insights, Bill Shiell distills some of the hard-won wisdom—and even joy—that can be gained from the failures, losses, and disappointments we inevitably encounter in life. I can imagine this is an invaluable book to read not only before we experience significant loss, but most especially to re-read during it.

—David Graybeal
Author of *Faith in The West Wing:
The Portrayal of Religion in a Primetime Presidency*
and *Bethlehem: An Advent Journey*

Someone once wrote, "God never wastes a hurt." For those who have hurt and then have grown in grace, those words are life-giving. Bill Shiell not only understands those words, but he also invests his hurt in people every day. Bill's wisdom that we can "learn from just about every failure" is a balm to the soul of one, like me, who has experienced loss. The book is life-altering for those of us who can acknowledge loss and invest our "hurt" in the lives of others. The spiritual exercises he outlines are worth the price of the book and more.

—Marvin Cameron
Senior Pastor, First Baptist Church
Kingsport, Tennessee

Bill's book *Losership* presents a new viewpoint on life for teenagers and adults. Experiencing "failure" can be especially challenging in a society that values achievements. This book redefines the concept, encouraging readers to embrace "losership" as a mark of faithfulness. I only wish I had this book during my time as a youth minister!

—David John Hailey
Senior Pastor, First Baptist Church,
Oak Park, Illinois

*To the Oak Room Herd
of Christ Church
Class of 2025*

*A person who loses his life for my sake
and the sake of the gospel will save it.*
Mark 8:35

Also by *Bill Shiell*

Reading Acts: The Lector and the Early Christian Audience

Sessions with Matthew

Delivering from Memory: The Effect of Performance on the Early Christian Audience

Acts (Preaching the Word)

Sessions with Exodus

*Ezekiel (*Annual Bible Study)
Teaching Guide and Study Guide

Contents

Preface	1
Chapter 1: The "Life 360" Plans I Have for You	11
Achievement Christianity	13
Symptoms of the Achievement Virus	14
Half-truths	14
Sadness	15
Material Blessings	15
Platitudes	16
Comparison	16
Anger and Rage	17
Control	17
Surveillance	18
Boredom and Escape	19
Stuck and Drifting	20
The Threshold of Joyful Christianity	20
Chapter 2: Lose Your Life	23
Jesus's Family and Education	24
Change Is Better	26
Suffering as Life	26
A Vision of Loss	28
Heaven's Portal	28
Earth's Portal	30
Standing at the Portal	30

Chapter 3: Learn from Loss	35
Role Models	36
The Successful Loser	38
Professor Failure	38
Chapter 4: Failure Class	43
Six Lessons from the Disciples' Classroom	43
Sit with the Loss in Jesus's Presence	43
Ask Jesus to Show You Your Role in the Failure	45
Pray Through and Name Your Emotions	46
Testify to Your Loss	48
Grieve the Loss of the Life You Thought Was Yours	50
Rise Transformed because of the Experience	52
Chapter 5: Think Like a Beginner	55
Prepare to Play	56
Paul and Timothy's Thinking from Prison	57
Watch Out for the Haters	57
Flush the Accomplishments	58
Focus on Jesus	58
Track Your Progress	59
The Loser's Staircase	61
Chapter 6: The Loser's Circle	67
A Place to Begin	71
Chapter 7: Characteristics of Joy	77
Obedient	78
Adventurous	78
Endurance	79
Attentive	79

Prayerful	80
Quietly Confident	80
Chapter 8: Return to Joy	**83**
Share in the Joy	86
Joseph and Pharaoh	87
Respond to Crises	88
Chapter Summaries for Group Discussions	**95**
Resources for Further Study	**101**

Preface

Ash Wednesday 2023 was a life-changing day for me. I was attacked online for my leadership style at a place and with people I loved at Northern Seminary. During nearly twenty-five years of faithful service in church-related ministries, I had never experienced anything like this.

That same day opened the door to a new beginning. I arrived at church to receive ashes, and two men from my small group came too. They did not know what was going on. I would later tell them the story, but they were just present with me and I to them. We received ashes, and I imposed ashes on them, and I grieved silently.

Life is unfair, especially when played out in the court of public opinion. Up to that point on Ash Wednesday, Northern Seminary and I were flying high. The Board of Trustees gave me great annual reviews. We were fully accredited. We were blessed to have an amazingly gifted faculty whom I admired and learned from. Our board pushed and challenged me to think and operate the seminary with a business mindset. I grew so much from their wisdom and friendship. We had a hard-working staff who developed innovative programs that benefited the church. Our students were the kind of pastors I wanted to learn from, and I enjoyed teaching them. Some of my favorite memories of Northern are hosting these students in our home and teaching on pilgrimages to Israel. These students reinvigorated my call to ministry and taught me so much about life and faith. Our givers cared so deeply about the future of the church and were excited about the growth and development in our students' churches. We received more donor support than before to advance our mission. We reinvented our model to attract more students worldwide and reduce student debt. Our previous two graduating classes were our largest in 60 years. Ironically, in October 2022, the trustees and faculty passed an update of our mission, vision, values, and standard of conduct. We addressed how to prevent the harmful effects of social media and the need to speak kindly, truthfully, and respectfully to one another. In six years, the organization had gone from floundering to flourishing.

My strengths also came with weaknesses and blind spots. I was a demanding leader who challenged the status quo. I valued accountability and follow-through for students and givers. I operated at a high tempo because of Northern's financial situation and my fear of failure. I am not the person described online. I was determined not to let Northern suffer the same fate as many other Christian institutions today. Our mission was way too critical to the church to let it die. However, my management style created an unsustainable level of anxiety in the institution; and I was unable to slow down and build the trust needed for long-term leadership.

The Board of Trustees wisely commissioned an independent investigator to examine concerns about my management style, and I welcomed her expertise and insight. I received encouragement, prayer, and support personally, pastorally, and professionally. However, by the time this process was finished, the damage had already been done. I voluntarily resigned in March. Soon thereafter, I resigned as an elder at my church. It was time for me to step away, examine where I was wrong, take responsibility for my actions, grieve the loss, ask God what the world needs from me, and forgive the people who harmed me.

I recognize that my commitment to leadership—even in Christian institutions—comes with a sacrifice and cost. Much like parenting, service with Christians exposes one's weaknesses and strengths. Unfortunately, we must wait for humiliating moments like these to learn the vital role of loss and failure. Jesus made suffering the centerpiece of his charge to Simon Peter in the Gospel of Mark—"A person who loses his life for my sake and the sake of the gospel will save it" (Mark 8:35). But if we're going to save our lives through loss, when and how do we teach and understand the critical role that losing plays?

We need to lose. We learn not just from the papers we get back and how they are graded, or just the ball game we were sure we would win; we must experience suffering and loss to live. We must surrender how we thought our lives would be, including our false motives, pride, and power. Since my resignation, I have now heard from several former leaders who are now part of a "club we never thought we would join." I empathize better with others I knew previously who were also subject to false accusations. Many pastors I know experienced something similar during the COVID-19 pandemic and have accepted callings into other forms of ministry. I respect their decisions.

We also need leaders. We look to them to point the way, name our pain, synthesize and analyze complex challenges, and show up when no one else will be present. We need leaders to develop a different kind of mindset about leadership. We need them so we can learn from people that Jesus emulated.

I am writing this book for the students who showed up at the Ash Wednesday service and keep showing up to church on Sunday evenings and in each other's lives. These students are just starting the journey: high school and college graduates who will suffer loss and failure. They will be fired, laid off, and resign when they think they are at the top of their fields. They will do the one thing I was told never to do—quit without another position waiting. They will not get into graduate school, even though they have been on the achievement road for a long time. They will be canceled online and face humiliation in ways we can never imagine.

Some of this will happen because American Christians will lead the charge to cancel them. These students are mega-talented, blessed, and privileged; they are cool, fun, and know how to win. They likely could do that anyway. But they are on the threshold of choosing a different way to survive—they want to live Jesus's way.

I am not writing this book to teach them how to avoid setbacks or loss, nor am I suggesting that if you master these principles, you too will be the president of a seminary one day. This is not a path to American-style success. I am writing to help you prepare to learn from suffering. For those who have not been through a life-altering setback, I am also writing to offer things you can say to people whose lives have been disrupted.

According to Bruce Feiler, most people will go through what he calls a "lifequake" about every eighteen months.[1] This is a planned or unplanned loss that disrupts their world, from death in the family to divorce to job loss to a relocation. We have been going through these things, and we will continue to do so. We cannot stop them or work around them; these lifequakes are embedded into the core of who we are and what we are to do about that.

We can run from them, try to control them, or do as the New Testament proposes: expect the lifequakes and learn from them. Failure is our teacher, a discipleship tool that Jesus, Paul, Timothy, and everyone else in the New Testament had at their disposal. Many Jewish, Greek, and Roman teachers and philosophers endured failure. Socrates, Seneca, and other ancient philosophers embraced loss. We will draw from their experiences and notice how Jesus's unique contribution helps us understand what to do with our losses.

Losses form us into who we are and train us in something I have called *losership*—not leadership. Leadership training is a prolific American industry. The idea captivates our imagination and discipleship programs from church to parachurch. American Christians are obsessed with leaders. Churches are shaped around cultivating, nurturing, growing, and training people to be at the top of a ladder. Despite the warnings across religious traditions against reaching for the top, we push people to want to be captain, president, or chairperson.

Losership offers a path through a different door. This is the journey with a group of people who find deep joy at the bottom of the roller coaster through living the adventure with Jesus. We are graduating these students in a way that does not require them to choose the perfect college major or career path. Jesus is the way, truth, and life (John 14:6), no matter what direction we choose, and he is with us on our journeys. He invites us to build a portfolio of options and skills to choose from, utilizing a library of content from the archives of Scripture, and learning from the one thing these characters had in common—suffering.

I write from a place of reflection on my ministry, realizing that some of the best work in God's kingdom and society generally comes when surprise, disaster, and the unplanned overwhelm us. I grew up on the Gulf Coast of Florida, where we planned for hurricane season, tracked storms, and prepared for the worst. Sometimes the worst came. But we found the most remarkable people, projects, and mission opportunities during those crises. Through loss, we refocused, reconnected, and transformed our experiences.

Our future as Christians living in America depends on inviting more people on this journey. What if the answer to the problem of nurturing someone to be an authority figure is not training more people to be at the head of the class? What if the people we are looking for aren't leaders at all? What if we are actually looking for "losership"? Most of the people who have influenced my life would not consider themselves to be leaders. They were the left out, marginalized, overlooked people. They were people whose fathers died or whose mothers left. They were the ones who came from and out of a place of loss. They had a "Jonah experience" where they ran from their responsibilities. Someone or something in them died, and they were finally brought to the shore to do what they were summoned to do.

This book is also for the mentors, parents, and strangers lingering in the hallway. They appeared unsuccessful, did not make the varsity team, and did not have social networks or capital. This is for all of you: know that you are our role models for life. You teach us the patterns of behavior that we need to live good lives. We aren't the experts; according to Jesus, you are. I also empathize with parents who had an excellent plan for their children and provided them with a great education, and their children chose a different way to live their adult lives. This book is for those who cannot send happy family Christmas cards and avoid Facebook during the holidays. Your children have not followed your plan, but God is still with them.

This book is for people who want to do something about the loneliness crisis in America. The surgeon general now calls loneliness a public health crisis.[2] Loneliness is at the root of the violence we see play out in schools, churches, and town squares. According to Jillian Peterson and James Densely, teenagers who carry out mass shootings have no friends and are looking to belong. Many of them have attended church at least once. In despair, they attempt to die by suicide while taking out others.[3] There is no justification for gun violence or even for someone owning an automatic weapon outside of the military without training and licensing. If someone had cared enough to intervene, we might have been able to stop some of these massacres. Leaders are often trained to look for leaders—not losers. If we want to do something about the character crisis in America, though, we will start looking around the social spaces of our lives—in gyms, schools, workplaces, restaurants, and virtual spaces—and leaning in, reaching out, and making friends with those who are left out.

Losership pays close attention to those in the back of the room, those with mid-level or lower grades. It looks for those without much charisma who are left out of most discussions or have anger management issues. Losership looks for the ones drifting in the hall, acting out, misbehaving, and disrupting the youth group. Losership befriends people labeled as misfits not to get them to fit in but to lean in, learn from, and invite them into an abundant relational life.

Here's what we can learn from them. To gain our lives, we must lose what we think makes us and others successful. We must learn to give up what made us leaders in the first place—the praise, glory, fame, recognition, and titles. Success, as defined by the educational system, is more money, a bigger house, an excellent network, and more significant opportunities to succeed. But losers understand that life was never about those things to begin with. When you don't have many things in the first place, you don't need to worry about gaining more things. Instead, connect to more friends, deepen your relationships, and serve one another.

We also need to give up looking to those with titles, degrees, platforms, and published books as the only ones with wisdom. As we discover in Scripture, and the life of Jesus especially, it's the blind, the disabled, and the dying who teach us best how to live joyfully.

These losers think about eight virtues that are at the core of their being, and their decisions seem to flow naturally from their lives: qualities that are true, honorable, just, holy, pleasurable, reputable, virtuous, and praiseworthy. Yes, they do tend to show up in similar places. They attend funerals, serve meals, welcome refugees, and let refugees welcome them. Some of them have faced the threat of imminent death, and others have been fired and left out. Some eventually gain positions of authority, but most good ones use those positions to help lift others.

Losers do not operate in silos. They are in communities, and the communities shape and form them into who they are. They hold them accountable. Losership is not an "anything goes" mentality. It is an understanding that I will give my all and allow myself to make mistakes, learn from them, and surrender what I have lost. I believe that the best life is as detached as possible from personal ambition and solely focused on the one priority—to love God with all my heart and love my neighbor as I love myself. And let's admit many people do not love themselves today. We experience it at schools, at work, in families, and in neighborhoods; these people take out their shame, guilt, and fear on others publicly, online, and privately where they live, work, and worship. If we work hard, we can truly learn to love ourselves and grow into a new journey of losership.

A book like this would not be possible without the extraordinary people in my life. I want to thank my wife Kelly and my sons Parker and Drake for their undying support through this time of grief, sadness, and bewilderment. We wept together and stayed with each other. We shared a lot of long walks and swim meets as we asked together what God wanted us to know and do because of these events.

My late mother, Sara, was a constant source of strength. She died at the age of 90 just before this book was finished.

PREFACE

I thank my pastor, Rev. Dr. Daniel Meyer, for his wise counsel. Several close friends guided me on this journey and kept in touch with me. I am grateful to Matthew DuVall, Marvin Cameron, Nicholas Hughes, David Graybeal, Pete Stearns, David John Hailey, Lee Fox, Mark Davies, Steve Reitmann, Jeff Madsen, Josh Carney, Shaun King, Daniel Headrick, John Roland, Adam Greenway, Matt Cook, Kyle Reese, Brent Beasley, Gerald Dew, Suanne Camfield, Tracey Bianchi, and Jeaneane Payne. Your messages, calls, and simple notes like "I'm praying for you" have sustained me.

Two groups have also been important in my healing. Lyndall Farley has facilitated a sabbatical group and offered fantastic feedback to me on this manuscript. Jeff Madsen chairs the board of Convene CT79, and he graciously invited me to serve as a volunteer anchor member this year. Thank you to Jeff Crosby, President of the Evangelical Christian Publishers Association, who first read this book proposal and encouraged me to share these lessons.

I am grateful to my friends at Smyth and Helwys, especially Keith Gammons for his steadfast support, feedback, and willingness to publish this manuscript.

Seven years ago, our family pastor, Dr. Steve Noble, allowed me to attend "Camp Cow" in 2017 and asked me to serve in the church's middle school ministry. He would not let me quit in 2019 and 2020 when I did not know how to reign in my rowdy bunch. Indeed, I made many mistakes, and now I'm glad I did.

I am dedicating this book to that same group—fifteen high school guys who meet in the Oak Room at Christ Church on Sunday evenings. I have had the privilege of loving on, learning from, and letting them love me while we have lived in Chicago. They sat with me on Ash Wednesday, heard my experiences, texted me supportive messages, and continued to throw shoes at the ceiling while we shared our stories.

They formed a basketball league and taught me how to coach a sport. Some of them also read and listened to the first drafts of this manuscript. We studied these concepts together on Thursday evening through Google chat calls. They will graduate soon, and this is my graduation gift to them. As they embark on the journey, they will have a template to refer to and a guide for the next phase. When they continue to make mistakes, they will know that defeat is a sign they are learning to be closer to the Lord.

If we are going to be present in this world as believers, we first need to give up the plans we have and be ready for the adventure ahead. In chapter 1, I will explain how we got here in this current environment. What made us loathe losing so much? Then, in chapter 2, we will look at Jesus's vision that he gave his disciples and the teachable moment he brought to their failure. In chapter 3, we will discover role models we need for the journey and then enroll in "Professor Failure's" class on the topic in chapter 4. In chapter 5, we take eight steps to reframe our mindset about failure, and in chapter 6, we form a losership circle to guide us through the process. We will learn in chapter 7 the characteristics of the joyful life we seek. Finally, in chapter 8, we will discover what the journey of losership has been about—the same joy that Jesus will share with us when he returns.

This book's format is designed for graduates and their small groups to use together to ask discussion questions. I have provided a few resources to get you started. The best lessons, however, will come as you journey through your failures.

Chapter 1

The "Life 360" Plans I Have for You

For I know the thoughts and plans I have for you, says the LORD. (Jeremiah 29:11)

My grace is sufficient for you, for power is made perfect in weakness. (2 Corinthians 12:8)

Many graduates today think they need a clear plan for their lives. I was one of them. Twenty-five years ago, long before the current graduates were born, I graduated from Baylor University at the top of my class. I assumed I would be immediately called to a church to serve as a senior minister. After interviewing at twenty-five country churches, my wife Kelly and I decided to stop counting how many times we heard the word "no." Little did I know that experience would prepare me for the surprising twists of this latest adventure. One of my pastors, Aaron Foster, gave me an image to describe my feelings—going down the Colorado River in a raft without an oar. In spring 2023, I lost control and was trying to stay in the "boat." My family and I had experienced something similar (with real oars) on a family vacation to Rocky Mountain National Park in 2016. Now, we were living through the metaphor together.

How could I have misunderstood the routes we can follow along the journey of the Christian life? As a young Christian, I was taught and believed that God laid out a plan for my life (Jer 29:11). I assumed wrongly that this plan followed a straight path (Prov 3:6). If I followed God's directions, God would lead me to something more fulfilling and successful and include a pay increase. Little did I know, and I am still learning, that "the path," "the plan," and my expectations for the future were wrong because I had misinterpreted the Bible.

When I first memorized Jeremiah 29:11, I interpreted this verse like many American Christians do. We think we are supposed to have a definitive, successful plan. I preached that "God has *a* plan for your life," but I knew inside that this interpretation was wrong.

The prophet Jeremiah preached this idea when the enemy, the Babylonians, took his people, the Jews, into exile. This experience could not have been the intention of a loving God. In hindsight, exile was one of several routes the people could follow. If God's chosen people from the Old Testament had multiple options, we have multiple options too. Every path is neither direct, straightforward, nor upward. But God is with us no matter where we go or where our lives take us.

Something similar has happened to American Christians. A vision of success has infected our operating systems like spiritual ransomware. This virus has turned what was joyful Christianity into a hateful, angry religion of self-righteousness, bitterness, and isolation. You would likely interpret the Bible differently if you were born in Cairo. Instead, you came into our world here, in America. The good news is that you are not alone and are not the first to confront the virus. This disease is not a problem you need to fix. However, you can learn to spot it as you take the next steps. You can also take pity on those infected by it and develop immunity against it. I want you to dare to walk through the doorway to joy. To do this, you must know what prevents you from getting there independently.

Achievement Christianity

Christian success is often defined today by more money, a bigger house, a more extensive network, and opportunities to succeed. In American Christianity, I call this "achievement Christianity." The ancient Israelites had a similar concept.[1] The premise goes that God will reward us materially and in our families for doing good and punish us for doing wrong. We have adapted that idea in our American Christian contexts: "God wants me to be successful and will reward me accordingly. If there are setbacks and struggles, these are only part of the pathway to success."

The Old Testament character Job, who lost everything despite doing nothing wrong, discovered that his so-called "friends" loved this idea of achievement. Jesus's disciples did, too. They assumed that following him would earn them a seat at the "right and left" in heaven (Matt 20:23; Mark 10:40). They wrongly thought that "the pursuit of happiness" ended with God's favor. We think that too. What makes us happy is what makes our parents happy. What makes us happy is what God wants.

If this is a biblical idea, then what's wrong with it? The Israelites tried it, and many American Christians have pursued it. But the virus prevents us from enjoying the life Jesus offers us. Let's look at the symptoms of the Achievement Virus and see if we spot any of them in our lives.

Symptoms of the Achievement Virus

If a person has a fever, congestion, body aches, and other symptoms, we know they likely have a cold virus. There are also symptoms common to the "achievement virus." When we have any of the following symptoms, we must examine how we think about Jesus.

Half-truths

The notion that God rewards those who do good is only partly correct. In fact, it is not even half right. We must read the entire narrative of Scripture to understand that Jesus did not teach this way of living. He did not have the technology we have today. But he did understand the achievement-reward mindset, and he saw the way it wreaked havoc on the people of his day. Back then, people turned to politics, the state, the Hebrew Bible, and many other places to figure out the best way to solve their world's problems. They imposed their view of this God on Jesus, hoping he would become a political, military, and materialistic savior for them, too.

Jesus did say that we would be blessed, but not materially; we would be blessed virtuously, with a community, loving each other along the way. God would use us to accomplish what God wants. God would use the unsung people behind the scenes, people that you and I might call "losers" because of the achievement culture we live in.

If we do receive material benefits or work hard for the future, then God wants us to share our material blessings with others. In other words, this is how we save our lives from empty happiness: by doing something that Jesus, Paul, Esther, and several other people we will meet did. We will continue to surrender our need for achievement, see Jesus's vision, and respond to the needs of people around us. We will lose what we thought was supposed to be our best life for a much more joyful existence.

Many great Christians I know prayed, studied God's word, served, and surrendered, and they still had plenty of problems. Their children got cancer, their parents died, and they lost. This was not because of anything they did wrong. They weren't suffering the consequences of bad behavior. They were taking the risk of life itself.

Sadness

The second symptom of the achievement virus is the deep sadness of people who have lived the achievement-reward model of the Christian life. In my experience, achievement Christianity only produces people who are more anxious and stressed because they worry that their accomplishments will be taken from them. The achievements and merits do not offer the kind of "peace that passes understanding" that this lifestyle promised (see Phil 4:7). Instead, there is always a desire to do more. In the worst-case scenarios, if anyone is considered a threat, they are marginalized and dismissed.

Material Blessings

Because we follow Jesus, we often receive multiple blessings. Our church, friends, family, and others exemplify Jesus's love to us. American Christians especially also enjoy vacations, careers, homes, healthcare, and choices many others worldwide cannot access.

Those blessings can signify that the achievement virus is trying to hold us hostage. The Bible does not condemn material wealth, but Jesus warns us about becoming attached to material things.[2] Our relative lack of significant problems compared to the rest of the world dulls our hearts. Freedom to worship, our beautiful facilities, and full-time church staff can make us think that church is a Christian concierge service. We have Young Life, a youth group, apps, services, and so much content. We have Jesus and his teachings at our fingertips. The blessings we have are symptomatic of a more profound truth.

Platitudes

Sometimes, even well-meaning Christians with setbacks default to achievement Christianity to explain away their suffering. Achievement Christianity markets itself well; many Christians think this is the only story to tell. They resort to saying platitudes like these:

- In a time of loss, "God has a better plan." Or "I know God has something better for you in your next job."
- When a loved one dies, "The angels in heaven must have needed them more than we did."
- To a child whose parent dies, "You're now the man/woman of the house."

These bromides ignore the good relationships formed and work accomplished in the past. To children and families, they become curses, making them think they have not lived up to what God wanted them to do—or, even worse, that they have not done enough to receive the everlasting life God wants for them in this life and in the life to come.

Comparison

When we suffer, we often compare our circumstances to those of others. TikTok and Snapchat feed off the hunger for people to belong and be seen. When we are practicing achievement Christianity, we compare our lives to the lives of others, and we are never enough. We always feel that we are missing out on a party, an award, or a specific body size or shape.

Anger and Rage

The sixth symptom of the achievement virus is something we experienced during and after the COVID-19 pandemic. We are a world deeply angry with each other. We love to take out our anger by becoming a mob scene. During COVID, we watched many people in our world suffer, whether physically from a virus or mentally because of the lockdown. The lockdown also revealed intense racial tension in the US.

What happened after the most devastating days of the pandemic? After being behind closed doors, we gradually reemerged, depending on where we lived. But we continued to drift farther apart and retreat to our own worlds. We filled the space between with more significant threats, terror, and strife. Many Christians have been the primary instigators of this hatred. One look at social media shows that Christians have perfected something commonly called "cancel culture," which is fueled by the same resentment that Jesus warned us about in the Sermon on the Mount. It's not enough to see someone face the consequences of their behavior or allow time for dialogue, reconciliation, and a fair process. Christians want to presume guilt publicly, scorn, shame, and ban people personally and professionally.

Control

The anger and rage in us fuel the seventh symptom. Control and self-centered power are versions of something we naturally need. Every American Christian generation wants to feel that they control their circumstances. We sing and declare that God is in charge, but it is implied that God has also delegated to us the ability to control the circumstances of our lives—down to the details. We call that symptom micromanaging one's life, and sometimes even one's parents are involved.

From where we live to our job to the grades we receive, we love to steer the path toward what we perceive to be the good things and ignore the lessons we can learn from the bad. A sense of agency is a normal human desire. Everyone needs to feel some ability to choose for themselves. Autonomy without dependency on others is anarchy, and dependency without autonomy is laziness. When we try to be in control of every detail or depend on others to do the same for us, we become obsessive or stuck.

As I mentioned earlier, the feeling of being in the "oarless riverboat" exposed some of my deeper challenges. When faced with the unexpected, I became more hands-on. I worked harder, moved faster . . . and only contributed further to the problem. I reached the point where helplessness was the only certainty.

Surveillance

The eighth symptom monitors us to ensure we are on the right path. My generation inherited what has commonly become known as the "helicopter parent." Some of our parents came to every ballgame, watched closely, cheered us on, and even showed up at college to ensure we were fine. Reacting against their late-boomer, early-buster parents, they wanted to show their emotional support for everything. These helicopter parents quickly became lawnmower parents.[3] They showed up for everything, blazed a trail, and ensured we could succeed. If you have participated in the Christian organization Upward, you know their motto is "Everyone is a winner." They were the Christian version of the participation trophy, and they perfected it.

Today, because of the power of technology, the most insidious form of achievement Christianity among my generation is "tracking parents." Using the Life 360 app or similar tools, we think we know our children's whereabouts, even though many of them have figured out a workaround. We are tracking to close the gaps that technology has created between us. We grieve the loss of conversation and fill it with more apps.

We have "Ring" doorbell systems to keep people out and "Life 360" to discover where our loved ones are and hopefully prevent hardship. Instead of making us more confident and trusting, surveillance makes us more anxious, drives a wedge between people, creates more significant conflicts, and lowers communication. As Costica Bradatan notes, "By trying to be perfect and be everything, we miss the chance to achieve what might be within our reach."[4]

Boredom and Escape

The ninth symptom, boredom, seems like a benefit on the surface. We might think boredom is the absence of work and the pleasure of accomplishment. Boredom is actually a choice that goes back as far as Jonah and the young guy named Eutychus in the book of Acts. They both tried to escape from reality, turn off the mental switch, and numb themselves to their world.

When we see the problems in our world—war, poverty, disease, climate disasters, mass shootings—we want to turn off the switch too. We have active shooter drills for public and private schools, and I remember wanting to talk about a mass shooting one night at church with our group. The common sentiment was that so many were happening that we had become numb to them.

To get away from reality, we try to escape. Not all choices have the same consequences, but every one of them is an escape from reality. Students and adults today are playing video games, doom scrolling, watching porn, gambling online, consuming substances, drinking alcohol, and engaging in fantasy sports. Tired of being micromanaged and pushed to achieve more, we try to escape the world instead of facing reality—only to find ourselves stuck and drifting.

Stuck and Drifting

This boredom leads us to the tenth and final symptom: stuck and drifting. After being tracked and monitored, you'd think we could quickly get out of the ditch. Unfortunately, the opposite happens. Surrounded by surveillance and numb, we become rudderless and adrift. Not able to live up to the achievements we witnessed in our parents, or thought we wanted for ourselves, we wait helplessly as victims of a situation where we blame others and wonder why this is happening to us.

The Threshold of Joyful Christianity

There must be a better way to live. I have discovered that there is another way to live Jesus's way, and it has set me on a different kind of joyful journey. Ironically, it has been there all along, and Jesus described it in the heart of his ministry. I ignored it, looked past it, and wondered how I could use it in "the plan."

In the past twelve months, as my "plan" collapsed under me, the oars fell off, and no one was guiding me, I learned more about what Jesus meant. I began to live in something that we call a liminal space, a threshold between one phase of life and the next. It is as if Jesus has done for us what he promised in Revelation: "Behold, I have set before you an open door, which no one can shut" (Rev 3:8, RSV). We need to decide to walk through this doorway.

For those about to graduate into the next phase of life, our country is sorting out what kind of people we will be for the next generation. There are many ways to live through this liminal time, and I suggest that Jesus provides a way to live this life joyfully. By God's grace, you already have everything you need. You live fully, learn more about where you are, and be ready to walk through the next door. This step will come not because you planned for it but because life threw the unplanned at you. You will respond because you are already grounded in a faith full of adventure, joy, curiosity, wonder, and love.

My first challenge for you is to stop planning. It's okay to have no clue what's next. I certainly do not. Remember the 25 country churches? That was just a dress rehearsal for this season of life. Since March 2023, I am still receiving more "nos" than I can count.

I have learned, however, this sense of uncertainty is not rejection. It's the feeling of standing on the threshold of a new, joyful relationship with Jesus. He wants us to walk through the doorway. To do so, we must let go of the life we thought we wanted.

Discussion Questions

1. What is "achievement Christianity," and where do you see it today?

2. Why is "achievement Christianity" like a virus? What does it do to us?

3. Have you seen or experienced any of these symptoms?

4. Read the story of Eutychus in Acts 20:7-12. How is he similar to the biblical character Jonah?

Chapter 2

Lose Your Life

> *The door is open to go through*
> *If I could, I would come, too*
> *But the path is made by you*
> *As you're walking, start singing and stop talking*
> *Oh, if I could hear myself when I say*
> *(Oh, love) love is bigger than anything in its way.* ("Love Is Bigger than Anything in Its Way," U2, lyrics by Adam Clayton, Dave Evans, Larry Mullen, and Paul David Hewson)

In 2016, I accepted a call to come to Chicago as president of Northern Seminary. Kelly and I had always thought we would be called to service overseas, but this felt like the "great adventure." We prayed about the decision as a family, reflected on our journey, and leaned into my original call: "Whom shall I send, and who will go for us, and I said, 'Here am I; send me!'" (Isa 6:9-10). Northern wanted to restore their campus and to train pastors for the church. They embraced women in pastoral leadership and were working on church-based solutions to racial injustice and reconciliation. I cared deeply about these issues.

When I arrived, things were not what I imagined. The campus was falling apart. Abandoned buildings were leaking water, costing us $10,000 per month. On the day I accepted the call, the chief development officer and CFO resigned. I arrived on February 29, 2016, in sleeting weather. My campus apartment was dark, dirty, and musty. The next morning, I awoke to fire trucks because there was a gas leak in the building. In April 2016, the new finance director informed me we had run out of cash. At this point, I almost went home. We had not sold our house yet, and we were not far from my mother or Kelly's parents. The decision to be the seminary president felt like a huge mistake.

Losing is unpopular in America. Nobody writes books on learning to fail better. There are also no manuals for dying seminaries, businesses, or organizations, especially when you're leading one. At the door of my apartment, I was learning to sacrifice expectations and lean into the unexpected surprises of leading in a time of decline. In hindsight, I came to Chicago not to learn to lead Northern Seminary but to learn to surrender myself to Jesus.

Microsoft Word treats "losership" as a typo. It is unrecognized in the English language. Unless they want to be well-positioned for a high draft pick, every professional sports team tries to win. If we experience suffering or loss, business leadership books treat them as a path to success. We call it "the comeback." I am proposing a different perspective. As you walk through the doors after graduation, you will find that joyful people have lost the trail, fallen off the map, left behind achievement, and embraced loss and suffering as a way of living. They find guidance for direction, meaning, and purpose through failure and humility. To understand this, we must turn to the master loser, Jesus, to watch how he treated loss with his disciples.

Jesus's Family and Education

Jesus came from a family of losers. As I wrote in my Bible study on Matthew, a glance at his genealogy reveals that his tribe consisted of the unknowns, the forgotten, the poor, and the oppressed.[1] They were the forgotten ones in Galilee, a home to revolutionaries mixed in with Gentiles who assumed the only path to success was a connection to one of the Herods. The Romans even had a rhetorical school teaching oratory for future lawyers, senators, and governors.

Jesus was born into a family that survived loss. Read his family tree in the Gospel of Matthew (1:1-18). You'll notice some people who would not pass a background check in today's world. Manasseh was one of the worst kings of Israel (2 Kings 21:1-18). Five mothers in the genealogy were rejected by their communities simply because of reputation, behavior, or both. Amazingly, Jesus's birth was scrutinized, and the ruler of the area, King Herod, felt threatened by his arrival.

Jesus also learned early on that suffering would prepare his disciples to live joyfully and wisely in the world. He knew from books in our Bible and stories not in our Bible but were popular in his day that God gives us discipline so we will turn to the Lord for wisdom (Wisdom of Solomon 6:7-12). This wisdom would allow them to endure suffering when attacked and persecuted (4 Maccabees 5:22-30; 7:31-34).[2]

These ideas shaped Jesus's thinking and the thinking of his disciples in such a way that they adapted them into their teaching. The writer of Hebrews and the apostle Paul did something similar. They viewed suffering as a teacher. They did not think God sent suffering to punish us or get our attention. They saw suffering as part of the contingency of life. To live, we will go through pain. Good and bad things happen to everyone. But God can use most suffering, loss, and failure to teach us how to live joyfully and wisely.

Think about a time when you broke a bone or had to wait for surgery. God did not cause your pain. Usually, injuries happen when we are enjoying our lives, and sometimes illness happens due to factors we still don't understand. That's the risk we take of living. The hard part is reframing the crisis points to become lessons. Our suffering, loss, and failure are a critical part of the curriculum of follow Jesus. They allow us to live more joyfully and make wiser decisions about our future. We will save our lives without needing achievement to make us successful. By joining Jesus on the journey, we are already there.

Change Is Better

I have hope and good news. Because of their experiences during the COVID-19 pandemic and changes in the education system, many graduates have naturally learned lessons from failure that they can apply today. They have coaches who give them feedback directly on the swim deck. When they have problems in class, they turn to each other on FaceTime or other apps to help solve the problem. Where a previous generation might label that behavior "cheating," this generation calls it "learning." When they want to play an instrument, they find a video on YouTube and friends to practice with. The classes of 2020 through 2025 have already mastered the only way to learn from failure—in a group. Jesus did something similar with his disciples. He used people others might perceive as failures as model citizens and problems in their ministry as teachable moments.

Suffering as Life

Let's begin with the passage from Mark 8:31–9:1. Take a moment to read this one a couple of times aloud.

> (8:31) Then he began to teach them that the Son of Man must undergo great suffering, and be rejected by the elders, the chief priests, and the scribes, and be killed, and after three days rise again. (32) He said all this quite

openly. And Peter took him aside and began to rebuke him. (33) But turning and looking at his disciples, he rebuked Peter and said, "Get behind me, Satan! For you are setting your mind not on divine things but on human things." (34) He called the crowd with his disciples, and said to them, "If any want to become my followers, let them deny themselves and take up their cross and follow me. (35) For those who want to save their life will lose it, and those who lose their life for my sake, and for the sake of the gospel, will save it. (36) For what will it profit them to gain the whole world and forfeit their life? (37) Indeed, what can they give in return for their life? (38) Those who are ashamed of me and of my words in this adulterous and sinful generation, of them the Son of Man will also be ashamed when he comes in the glory of his Father with the holy angels." (9:1) And he said to them, "Truly I tell you, there are some standing here who will not taste death until they see that the kingdom of God has come with power."[3]

Jesus takes his disciples to one of the signature places of achievement in Galilee—Caesarea Philippi. The name itself suggests "success": Caesar Philip. Appointed by the Roman emperor, Herod Philip, son of Herod the Great, ruled over this district for eight years. He built this area to commemorate Caesar's reign and increase tourism. He provided worship sites for Jews who wanted a synagogue and for Romans who wanted to worship the god Pan. They thought hell's gates were below the rock formation at Caesarea Philippi.

Jesus brought his disciples here to ask them what kind of vision they had for his ministry: "What is your vision of who I am and who God is? If you think I'm God, what kind of God am I?" Peter assumed that Jesus was a military king coming to conquer the Romans. When Jesus told him that he would instead suffer and die, Peter tried to rebuke Jesus. This wasn't the kind of Messiah Peter had in mind. Jesus needed to give these followers a vision—or a new mindset—about suffering: what it does, what it could teach them, and how they were to operate in the world. First, he gave them the principle: "For those who want to save their life will lose it, and those who lose their life for my sake, and for the sake of the gospel, will save it. For what will it profit them to gain the whole world and forfeit their life?" (vv. 35-36).

This powerful verse is Jesus's vision for his life and the life he wants for us. To live joyfully, he says we must lose the life we thought we would have and follow him into a different way of living. We must face what Peter faced by being wrong about Jesus and almost everything else. These ideas of God's kingdom do not come naturally, so we need a vision from Jesus that can change our minds, some role models, and practical direction.

A Vision of Loss

A vision is the picture or image we have for God's plans. Just as every artist has a concept in mind before she paints the portrait, so Jesus is our artist. He gives us a vision of what he wants for our lives using two portals—one from heaven and one from earth.

Heaven's Portal

First is the heavenly one. In one of the most awe-inspiring and wild events in Jesus's life, he takes his disciples Peter, James, and John to the top of an unnamed mountain, and there he glows. This is a heavenly liminal space, a concept I mentioned in chapter 1, a portal between one phase of life and the next and between heaven and earth. He reveals to the disciples what they could not see but he had known since he was a child. Jesus is in the presence of God because he is

God. Two figures who are signs of the end times stand beside him, Moses and Elijah. Their presence signals that the world as they imagined it is ending and a new era is beginning.

In the same way, Jesus will show us what to do and what will happen in our world. His arrival is the dawn of a new era and a new way of thinking about our lives. Peter, James, and John first react like they are on a fall retreat or at summer camp. They want this heavenly portal to be the destination. We want to stay in those heavenly places too. But in the moment when they are ready to camp out, God's voice describes the Father's relationship with Jesus: "This is my beloved Son; I am well pleased with him."

What was the transfiguration about? Think of this moment as a heavenly "transfer portal." When college athletes enter "the portal," they leave behind their scholarships at one school and hope that another school will match their financial aid. When the disciples enter this moment, they are taking a risk that Jesus is everything he says he is. They are leaving behind the life they thought they would have and turning to the vision Jesus has. Jesus isn't changing; the disciples are.

We are like these disciples. We need to see that Jesus's suffering had a purpose. He would die, be brutally persecuted at the hands of the Roman and Jewish leadership, rise from the dead, and return as a risen and ascended King. He is the King, but he is a King like we have never experienced. He shows the world through his sacrifice that suffering, loss, and service for others are the only ways to live significantly joyful lives. Achievement through power, fame, honor, and material possessions leads to more hardship, selfishness, pride, and anger.

Earth's Portal

That experience was fantastic for a mountaintop moment, but what about real life? As they descended the mountain, the disciples confronted real life face to face in their ministry. A father with a demon-possessed boy brought his son to Jesus. He was upset because Jesus's disciples could not drive out the demon. Even though Jesus had given the disciples authority to do so, they could not complete the task. The disciples were just as perplexed as the father. "Why couldn't we drive out the demon?" they asked. Their question was the answer Jesus was looking for. Despite the injustice and unfairness of a child ravaged by a demon, the moment became a teachable experience for the disciples. Jesus said, "This kind can only come out by prayer." Jesus then healed the boy and returned the child to his father.

Why did Jesus wait to take his disciples back to this boy and his father? He wanted to teach the disciples that their failure could help them trust in Jesus as the true and living God. The boy's father was the only person in the story who treated Jesus as God and, thus, was talking or praying to God. His prayer was simple, "Lord, I believe; help my unbelief."

Standing at the Portal

We begin to have a vision of joy when we go back through our stories. We look at our family history of loss and success. We look at our failures and learn from them. Review the symptoms of achievement Christianity in chapter 1. The disciples confronted the same issues in their lives. When we have those symptoms and realize we are losing, our mindset changes. When our minds change, our world can change. Our prayer to Jesus can be, "Lord, I believe; help my unbelief."

There are parts of Jesus we fully believe in and life situations where we have doubts and stray. He is there for all of it and invites us to trust him with our unbelief as much as our belief. How do we begin to do that? We start with a different kind of role model and measure a different kind of success.

I have drawn strength in this season by reflecting on my late father's journey. Before he met my mother, he was hospitalized in Chattahoochee, Florida, at the State Mental Hospital for several years with a misdiagnosed case of schizophrenia. My uncle, his brother, providentially met a psychiatrist who was experimenting with lithium. My dad was able to get out of the hospital, meet my mother, and then I was born. His life was not perfect, and he struggled to find work. I still have clippings of the classified ads he placed for himself in the early 1980s. By all accounts, he was the father who prayed, "Lord, I believe; help my unbelief."

Stories of struggle and failure have shaped who we are today as much as stories of success. Are you willing to find them, tell them, and then walk through the door of your own failures? When we realize the life we will live is not what we thought it would be, there is good news: the first step is *not to do anything*. The first step is to find examples to follow.

Discussion Questions

1. Reflect on the transfiguration scene. How did this event change the disciples' vision of Jesus' ministry?

2. What's your vision for the next year? What do you think is God's vision for you?

3. Think about some of the people you have turned to for guidance in your family. Are they celebrities or quiet people behind the scenes?

4. How did people in your past make you who you are today?

5. What are some "mountaintop" experiences you had in the past? What made them so special?

6. What lessons from these mountaintop experiences did you learn that you have never forgotten? Who were the people with you? What lessons could you carry into the future?

7. When have you failed at something you thought Jesus and the church trained you to do? How does the disciples' failure help you understand the purpose of that experience of loss?

8. What's your "transfer portal"? How can failure or change help you surrender? What do you need to leave behind?

Chapter 3

Learn from Loss

So the last will be first, and the first will be last.
(Matthew 20:16)

Most people have role models. Some of us follow YouTube or TikTok influencers, listen to their teachings, or track their sports progress. We may not say, "They're someone I want to be like one day," but we admire their lives and actions.

As we discovered in chapter 2, our role models may not get many likes or mentions in the Christian life. We admire them not because of their worldly success but because they enjoy life and have discovered most people don't realize until the end: we must lose the life we thought we would have to gain the one Jesus has already provided and wants us to have. To become the humans God created us to be, we must learn to appreciate the loss of control, the feeling of uncertainty, and the pain of suffering.

Jesus had role models, too, some living and some dead. They were the kinds of people the writer of Hebrews describes as a part of the "cloud of witnesses." They inspired Jesus to blaze a trail leading to joy that came through suffering. Read Hebrews 12:1-2:

> (1) Therefore, since we are surrounded by so great a cloud of witnesses, let us also lay aside every weight and the sin that clings so closely, and let us run with perseverance the race that is set before us, (2) looking to Jesus the pioneer

and perfecter of our faith, who for the sake of the joy that was set before him endured the cross, disregarding its shame, and has taken his seat at the right hand of the throne of God.

Did you notice the joy? That is Jesus's plan for you—a life filled with joy. This theme verse is at the heart of our church's ministry with middle schoolers. Our students are crazy, fun, and full of laughter, and they also get down to business simultaneously. They read the Bible, ask good questions, and disrupt others. They have modeled for me the thinking at the heart of losership. Our groups are unorganized, chaotic, unplanned, vibrant, and joyful. I also realized it took me fifty years to find a life of joy, so I do not want you to wait that long to understand what you already have and can experience the rest of your life.

Role Models

I was fortunate to have many examples to follow in church ministry. Still, the ones who had the most significant impact on me were not teaching in seminaries or pastoring large churches. When I pastored my first church in McGregor, Texas, one of the people who influenced me most was David Zacharias. We had a nursing home ministry, and I was responsible for preaching a message there each Wednesday morning. Admittedly, I was nervous and distracted by all the other things I needed to accomplish. David was one of our volunteers and set an excellent example for me. He was energetic, caring, and hospitable. He greeted residents, assisted them to the dining room for the service, and sat with them as they sang and I preached. David also had Down syndrome, a condition that only enhanced his ability to empathize and pastor these people.

Similar role models are found throughout the pages of Scripture. For instance, Esther, an ancient world version of a person caught in human trafficking, was a picture of this kind of suffering. With her people facing genocide by the Persians, her relative Mordecai intervened. He challenged her to risk her life to save her people. She used the same language with Mordecai that Jesus used with his disciples: "If I perish, I perish."[1]

When Jesus first began to gather disciples, he held up role models that looked like those in his biological family. They were likely not included in the Roman senate. They were poor in spirit, meek, merciful, pure in heart, humiliated, and persecuted. Jesus found them along the way for the disciples to learn from and emulate, especially when they disrupted the disciples' plans. Each one had experienced loss.

- A man named Bartimaeus lost his vision.
- A man named Jairus lost his daughter.
- A man on a mat lost the ability to walk.

The people responded differently to each one. The crowds often got in the way each time, but the "loser" arose because Jesus showed the person mercy and forgiveness.

- The disciples tried to silence Bartimaeus.
- In Capernaum, a crowd blocked the entrance to a home, and a group of people lowered a paralyzed man through a roof.
- Jairus broke through a crowd to interrupt Jesus, and Jesus went to the man's home.

Each one depended on Jesus to save them, no matter what the crowds thought. They had already experienced loss and suffering, so they were not worried about humiliation. They did not mind being told "no." In the paralyzed man's case, we are unsure if he wanted to be carried, but the carriers were willing to risk rejection to lower the man through the roof.

Each one experiences a resurrection in their earthly life. They "arise" in some way: they get up from their past, or the thing holding them back, leave it behind, and live a joyful life from then on. Notice I did not say they live an ambitious life full of achievement. They live a life that Jesus has touched. The losers have a greater understanding and vision of who Jesus is, what he is about, and what he can do for people.

The Successful Loser

Jesus holds up "losers" as successes. Jesus is always looking out for—and teaching the disciples to look out for—the lost sheep, coin, and sons (Luke 15:1-32). When a woman with an alabaster jar disrupts a dinner party where Jesus is a guest, the disciples reject her sacrificial gift. They want to use the money for people experiencing poverty. Jesus instead honors who the woman is because that is who he is. He loves people who provide abundantly, give extravagantly, and disrupt organized religious settings. Jesus prioritizes things that disrupt our plans, disturb the party, and create joy. He wants us to focus on those things too. A sign of Jesus's presence is usually our inability to gain control or devise a plan. When life leaves us helplessly looking for someone to save us, Jesus always shows up.

Professor Failure

Who and what can we learn from to help us start the journey to losership? Just as Jesus did with his disciples and his own life, he wants us to learn from the one thing we seek to avoid. Failure and loss are the best teachers. For instance, students talk about "that class." We were warned not to register for a certain course, and everyone told us not to take this or that professor for credit. A particular class would damage our GPA; ultimately, we might not get into law school, med school, or anything else. However, Professor Failure is the one teacher who can help us find joy.

Here's a secret, though. Failure is everywhere, even though people do not like to admit it. We are a nation of people who have lost everything—often unjustly. In the United States, we have entire generations of Black families who came from countries that sold them into slavery. Some of them migrated to the North, the Midwest, and the West only to find that they were continually oppressed. Irish families came after losing potato farms. Persecuted people from Vietnam, China, the Sudan, and more have flooded our shores. Migrants arrive even now who are persecuted for their faith and have lost their homes in war. Each failure is different, and each group and person has their own stories. We don't have to look far to find people who have experienced and continue to experience loss, and we can learn from them.

That, of course, is not the American dream. We are a society built on and surrounded by people who have made one goal their priority—to live better off than their parents did. That dream has become a curse for many, and it has undoubtedly infected a lot of Christian discipleship and preaching as well.

Failure, loss, and suffering can teach us something much different. As I mentioned in chapter 1, God does not cause most suffering. If we read through the Bible, there are about ten explanations for suffering. Most pain results from the gift and risk of living or from evil's presence in the world. We can't simply blame God for all of our problems. We know that through Jesus, God suffers with us when we hurt and does not cause our pain. When we hurt, God does too.

When I met with my counselor in 2019 about the situation at Northern Seminary, he showed me a different ministry model. He told me, "You were not called to Northern Seminary to fix Northern. Northern got itself into this mess on its own, and it's not your job to get it out. Your job might be to close it down and bless the past work. Your job is to be present with it, lead it as best you can, and hand it to the next person." That statement was like a healing balm for me. Later it also helped me examine my own reactions and motives, which I will discuss in the next chapter.

Another thing to remember is that not all loss and suffering result from failures on our part. If a child has cancer, no one has done anything wrong, and there is no one to blame. The disease is a loss but not a failure. If anything, the disease is often a sign of a failed world and a signal to us of why we need Jesus to return to make things right. I will share more on that topic later as well.

This is not a book explaining why we suffer; I will leave it to you and your peers to take a class that explores those issues. To discover a joyful life, however, I want us to think about a common thread to all forms of loss: *we can learn from just about every failure*, both our part in it (if there was a decision to be made) and the loss due to unjust and unfair behavior. Let's register for the "class" and see what failure must teach us.

Discussion Questions

1. Who are your role models, and what are some of their experiences of loss that you can learn from?

2. What areas of your life are you trying to fix? Is this your assignment or someone else's?

3. Failure can often leave us alone and isolated, but sometimes soul friends are there for us when we least expect it. Their support can be a source of comfort and strength during times of loss or suffering. Who has shown up for you during a time of loss or suffering?

4. When have you suffered an injury or illness and had to wait an extended period of time for healing? What did you learn?

Failure Class

All who exalt themselves will be humbled, and all who humble themselves will be exalted. (Matthew 23:12)

I am asking you to consider something your parents probably don't want you to attempt—failing. We parents love achievement, but I promise this class will eventually bring a deep well of satisfaction. When approached with the right mindset, failure can be a powerful tool for transformation and growth.

Six Lessons from the Disciples' Classroom

Jesus's disciples are joining us in failure class today. They are still perplexed, wondering why they cannot do what Jesus has taught and equipped them to do. As I mentioned in chapter 2, they could not heal a demon-possessed boy, and the boy's father was exasperated. This leads us to six lessons from Professor Failure.

Sit with the Loss in Jesus's Presence

Life teaches us to move on and move forward. Indeed, we do often need to keep going. However, in the Christian journey, Jesus meets us at the point of loss and summons us there as students. He and his cross, symbolic of his ultimate suffering and loss for us, meet us at the beginning of the journey. That is why Jesus took his inner circle to a high mountain. He wanted them to see early on what his life and ministry—and theirs—were all about. He wanted them to visualize what they were getting into and what he was trying to *get out of them*. He taught them that sacrifice, suffering, and loss were not something to be ashamed of, avoided, or controlled. This is not a tragic story but a glorious beginning to a life of joy.[1] We will not fully understand everything, but we can see what the process entails. Jesus is with us, guiding us through our failures and losses.

Pay attention to your emotional reaction(s) to overwhelming moments. Failure usually opens a wound or trauma from the past, allowing you to reflect on what is inside. The disciples were afraid, bewildered, and proud. They thought they could solve the problem, and they could not. They were helpless. We learn later that they were highly competitive, envious, and ashamed. All these emotions and more attempt to fill in the gaps left by loss. Watch for them, name them, and learn from them.

Also pay close attention to the people who have lost something or someone, like the father with his sick child. Learn to be present with them in their suffering. You are not there to fix the world and solve all the problems, but you are called to show up.

Jesus gives every believer one superpower: to show up personally in a crisis. This response becomes a directional marker for someone who has learned losership. At the bottom of the mountain, Jesus invited his disciples to return to a person whose problem they could not solve and be present with the father, even if they heard his humiliating public question: "Why could your disciples not do that?" By being in Jesus's presence and with others who follow him, we open ourselves to joy and grace.

In his book *The Cost of Discipleship*, the Christian martyr Dietrich Bonhoeffer wrote,

> Suffering is a joy and a token of his grace—Christ transfigures for his own the hour of mortal agony by granting them the unspeakable assurance of his presence. In the most brutal torture, they partake in the perfect joy and bliss of fellowship with him.[2]

In March 2023, for the first time in my life, I had to sit down with my anxiety and grief and process what I had been through. Like the disciples, I thought I had been trained to overcome these problems. Unlike the disciples, I quickly realized that my college and graduate degrees had not prepared me for this moment of suffering.

Ask Jesus to Show You Your Role in the Failure

The disciples took the next courageous step, asking Jesus what happened. In most losses, there is something we could have done differently or needed to do better to help transform our circumstances. The disciples tried to figure that out. Instead of blaming someone else or the Pharisees, they asked the decisive question, "Why couldn't we drive this out?"

Journaling is a powerful tool when you are exploring your role in a failure. At some point centuries ago, Christians decided to report and record their stories for us to have permanently on record. The Bible contains copies of these stories that we can reflect on. The journals of early Christians have become our template. One example is the book of 2 Peter. In 2 Peter 1:3-11, we read Peter's reflections about his experiences on this mountain with Jesus. The moment becomes a "last will and testament" for his church and generations of believers.

I recommend a journaling method my counselor suggested following my experience on Ash Wednesday. When Vietnam War veterans struggled with PTSD, James Pennebaker invited them to journal their emotions four days in a row for twenty minutes straight.[3] They reflected on their circumstances, looking for what they could learn, what meaning they could make, and how to transform the experience into something new. Then, they tore up the journal pages and put the circumstances behind them.

Through this process of journaling, I learned about my struggles with pride, control, comparison, fear, and tempo. In a crisis, I accelerated my pace. When our campus collapsed, I worked harder. During COVID-19, we worked hard to increase our enrollment quickly. We launched new programs. Despite the incredible success of these days, I was also contributing to over-functioning in an already stressed system. We had not fully recovered from the loss of our campus, and I had not paid close enough attention to the new virtual community. Even despite our successes, I was afraid that Northern would fail, and I too would be considered a failure. I was too involved in the details when we were in crisis mode. I needed to praise others more, shine the spotlight on others' success, and slow down.

Pray Through and Name Your Emotions

In your own process of journaling, feel and pray through your emotions, naming each of them. Avoid numbing your pain with distractions, substances, or busyness. People who are stuck and drifting are suffering a symptom of achievement Christianity (see chapter 1), which tells them to move on by numbing their emotions.

In this third lesson from the disciples' classroom, we slow down, avoid alcohol and other substances, turn off social media, take a Sabbath break, and dwell on our reactions. We identify toxic or negative emotions—hatred, unforgiveness, selfishness, disloyalty, despair, fear, and sadness. We practice what Brené Brown describes as the "reckoning." Knowing that we are emotionally hooked on something, we become curious about what we feel in our bodies. We breathe and ask ourselves if an unexpected situation warrants "freaking out" or venting to someone else what we are feeling.[4]

As I alluded to in the previous section, I had to reckon with my old pal, fear. Fear of the Lord can be an awe-inspiring emotion and response to God. Following my father's death, I tapped into a toxic fear to motivate me, and that often spilled out on others. It drove my decisions about everything from salvation to vocational decisions. Since we aren't promised tomorrow, I wanted to work urgently to make the most of every day. I lived like a travel cup full of hot coffee—without the lid. Whenever I was bumped, I spilled.

One habit that contributed to fear was venting. Usually, it added fuel to a stockpile of emotions. With the best intentions, I would bank all my feelings about church, family, and seminary until evening walks with my wife Kelly. We would use the walks to vent emotions with each other . . . and then wonder why we did not feel better after the walks! Buster, our dog, heard a lot of raw discussions. We need to stop and pray before we share our emotions or get vulnerable with anyone. This helps us evaluate what we have "stockpiled."[5]

We also need to look for healthy, others-focused emotions to guide us into the future. Courage replaces fear. Joy replaces sadness. Love replaces hate. Forgiveness replaces resentment. Giving replaces selfishness. Gratitude replaces entitlement. Faith replaces disloyalty. A starter prayer for this process is the prayer attributed to St. Francis of Assisi:

> Lord, make me an instrument of your peace:
> where there is hatred, let me sow love;
> where there is injury, pardon;
> where there is doubt, faith;
> where there is despair, hope;
> where there is darkness, light;
> where there is sadness, joy.
> O divine Master, grant that I may not so much seek
> to be consoled as to console,
> to be understood as to understand,
> to be loved as to love.
> For it is in giving that we receive,
> it is in pardoning that we are pardoned,
> and it is in dying that we are born to eternal life.
> Amen.

As Arthur Brooks notes, this process of prayer gets us ready to endure future struggles. We own our weaknesses, take off our masks, and embrace what really happened.[6] This kind of prayer prepares us for the next step.

Testify to Your Loss

We cannot transform failures by keeping them a secret. We must weave a story that allows us to "narrate our way into humility."[7] We need to own our story and discuss it with trusted friends. In this case, the disciples dialogued with Jesus about the failure and continued discussing the problem.

Look back and think about where you noticed God's presence in similar failures. How God worked back then is likely an indicator of what God will do again in the present and the future. As we tell others, we discover that we are not alone. Instead, we learn that other losers share similar experiences and need to hear our stories to help them. They can empathize, relate, and understand our journey. They might not have a solution to our problems, but they can help us know we are not the only ones.

As Bonhoeffer notes in *The Cost of Discipleship*, this is what Paul meant by "bear one another's burdens" (Gal 6:2). We often think that verse means helping each other in service. Bearing burdens also means sharing the weight of our sins and trusting a Christian friend to walk with us through the doorway of forgiveness into new life. Jesus bears that burden with us, including our temptations and the burdens others invite us to carry. My brother's and sister's burdens are their outward situations and their sins.

Every week in our small group, we take time for "happies and crappies." We share our highs and lows, often leading us down the trail of real pain. We have shared about family trauma, parents' jobs and marriages, broken bones, and social media shaming. My group has modeled what this kind of confession and transformation can do.

I rewrote my story of why and how I came to Chicago. Kelly and I once told each other I had come to Chicago to lead Northern Seminary. As I noted earlier, once I arrived, I realized things were much different than I expected. Our campus was falling apart; we experienced a lot of staff turnover; and many days, we wondered if we could make payroll. We even thought about closing the seminary.

Slowly, I began to testify to others. The former professor and author Parker Palmer once shared that he had to get to the point where he could tell his story without someone pulling him off the stage because he was too emotionally overcome. Thankfully, on Sunday evenings and Wednesday evenings, our student ministry allowed me to share my story. My Convene group and Sabbatical group helped me share lessons from the journey.

My counselor during my time at Northern and afterward helped me hear God's voice again and learn some hard lessons. God called us to serve and be the church so I could learn how to become a better Christian, father, friend, and leader from a group of sixth graders I am still with today. I have moved up with them as they have grown, and we have adopted a few others into our group along the way. My mom moved here in 2019 and lived out her days near us. The last two years have been especially meaningful for both of us. Kelly has now joined our church staff, experiencing a new calling in her life journey. We would have not had these experiences or formed these deep relationships without moving to Chicago.

Grieve the Loss of the Life You Thought Was Yours

Whenever life bottoms out and failure finds us, Jesus invites us to grieve. It is a powerful choice to acknowledge how life was and to surrender our plans that will never become what we wanted them to be. The memories, the people, and the past matter.

Grief can also be a powerful emotion that many of us have experienced. The Hinsdale Central High School classes of 2024 and 2025 lost a good friend and talented swimmer, Kendall Pickering, in a tragic car accident in North Carolina. Her life and legacy still ripple through our school, and each year we hold an annual swim meet and benefit in her memory. Last year, a boy named Sean Richards died tragically when a vehicle struck him outside of a car wash. Grief and tragedy are all around us and will continue to be.

Grief is an emotional and physiological response. It comes in many forms, primarily emotionally—either through anger or sadness—and can be expressed physically through tears and insomnia. But it can also be a holistic response that can happen anytime and for any reason. It has numerous symptoms and is seldom static.[8] One way we grieve is to ask ourselves what shape our grief is taking. Is it like a wave moving over us and carrying us out in the undertow, shattered glass in a million pieces, or the earth opening below our feet? Does our grief feel like a roller coaster or a transfer truck hitting us in an intersection?

As I mentioned earlier, the shape of my grief started like a river raft without oars. Then the shape changed. At times, I felt like the earth had opened underneath my feet. As a former pastor, president, and elder, I grieved the loss of the identity I had built my life around. Then, grief started feeling like deliverance from bondage and a journey into a wilderness adventure.

Naming the shape helps us understand that there are no sequential stages to grief. We process many emotions at once, and things take time to heal. The shape of our grief can help us understand how to keep moving and what the end might feel like. In my situation, reflecting on that first image, I know there are turbulent waters below me and in front of me, but eventually the waters will calm. It is important to follow the guide's instructions and stay in the boat of family, friends, church, and supporters.

The losses we choose to experience for good reasons are also times to grieve what we leave behind. Even in an exciting beginning, such as going to college or starting a new job, friends are lost. Relationships with parents change. If we are away at school for the fall semester, we miss out on things back home. This grief is just a preview of future grief to come.

Grief honors the memory of a loved one or a loved thing that is no longer the way it was. Grief heals the wounds of the past and allows us to say that this event, time, and place mattered. Every loss does not require a funeral, but we do not have to walk through loss alone. We can allow Jesus to weep with us.

We sometimes think about "what might have been." This is a place of grief, but it's not our final destination. We grieve the loss, but we cannot stay there. We must keep moving through the portal on the healing journey.[9]

Rise Transformed because of the Experience

As I mentioned in the previous chapter, what Bartimaeus, Jairus's daughter, and many others in the Bible did through loss is to rise. Jesus called them to "arise," and they did. They left behind their old ways and lived into the new way. They became part of a new community that faced reality and embraced uncertain plans with joy. They left behind achievements and understood that Jesus's presence and the society around them would be enough to sustain them.

In fall 2023 and winter 2024, I began to rise. I examined what gave me joy and what gifts God had given me to share with others. I volunteered as a mentor at an elementary school through KidsHope USA. I started announcing more swim meets, something that I loved to do. I substituted at two local high schools. Then, God began to open unexpected doors. Because I was more available to Drake and around the swimmers, a mom reached out to me about her son's spiritual journey. I met with Jeffrey, and he expressed a desire to follow Christ in believer's baptism. In May 2024, I held my first baptismal service in Lake Michigan. I'm confident I would not have had the experience of getting to know the Hou family without the time and availability of this season.

Failure can be an influential teacher if we allow that. But it will take more than a few role models and a class on what we can learn. Like any other class, what really matters is whether our lives change because of the class. Do we accept the grade or ignore the lessons and move on?

If we want to embrace losership, we need a new mindset about our current circumstances and our future. We must approach losing as if we're learning to play an instrument or a sport for the first time.

Discussion Questions

1. Failure is a great teacher, but people rarely want to go through that kind of experience. What failures have you had in the past, and what have you learned from them?

2. This chapter identifies six lessons in Professor Failure's class. Which ones have you tried? Which ones do you need to practice?

3. Transforming negative emotions to others-centered emotions is a powerful part of the process. Pray aloud the prayer of St. Francis of Assisi alone or together with other in a small group.

4. What is the shape of your grief over failure? Has it changed shape over time? Take a moment to draw that picture.

Chapter 5

Think Like a Beginner

> . . . *looking to Jesus, the pioneer and perfecter of faith, who for the sake of the joy that was set before him endured the cross, disregarding its shame, and has taken his seat at the right hand of the throne of God.* (Hebrews 12:2)

Congratulations! You've made it this far. Thank you for trusting me on the losership journey. This book is not your ordinary "graduation" manual. If you want to succeed by society's standards, you likely already have the resources, connections, and influence. But we've learned along the way that society's path to success eventually leads to feeling stuck, drifting, and disillusioned. That life instills a continual craving for more success. Nothing truly satisfies us, and ultimately, we lose our best lives.

We are working through an invitation to save your life. Only one thing is necessary—surrender the life you thought you would lead through achievement and take the risk of faith and adventure to discover a life of joy.

We have already learned that Jesus gave us a vision for this lifestyle. We did not need to set goals or write a strategic plan. We just needed to see and reflect on heaven and earth's vision, walk through the portal, and surrender to Jesus. We learned the most from the teacher no one told us to heed—failure itself.

Failure invites us into a different mindset about life. This new way of thinking will become a new way of joyful living. Certain passages in the Bible train us to develop a new mindset in our moments of failure. Paul and Timothy give us eight virtues to help us think differently about our lives.

Prepare to Play

Over the past few years, I have met several people who did something I would never do. They googled "how to play the guitar," found some YouTube videos, and a few weeks later they were playing the guitar! Wow. Lessons in losership are not offered on YouTube, but the mindset for learning an instrument is similar. We need to treat this process as if we are trying a new sport, hobby, or instrument.

The Bible calls this practice "repentance," literally changing our minds about how the world works and how we live. For Jews, that kind of new thinking could only come from developing and practicing new behaviors. The Romans, especially Stoics, believed they could think their way into a unique solution and that their bodies would eventually follow suit.

We need a bit of both thinking and practicing. We need to start thinking differently, reframing our circumstances and "plans," and then practicing our Christian lives the way a dancer works out or a swimmer swims. We do not prepare to play an instrument or new sport thinking we will be perfect. We simply prepare to learn. Amy Edmondson's studies reveal that we need "intelligent failures," plans and processes that we go into *expecting* to fail. We need a mindset that says, "Failure is permitted, and we have permission to reflect, learn, and grow. We must enjoy the uncertainty and prepare as if our lessons will inform the next steps."[1] This mentality requires practice.

Paul and Timothy's Thinking from Prison

For an example, we can look at what the apostle Paul and his sidekick Timothy endured in the book of Philippians. Paul was in prison, thinking and imagining the end of his life, and his young apprentice Timothy attended to his needs. Simultaneously, Epaphroditus, a good friend who almost died, delivered their mail and updated the Philippian church on Paul's condition many miles away. Epaphroditus also received money from the Philippians to take to another church in Jerusalem going through extreme difficulty.

Despite this support, Paul felt isolated and concerned about the future. He missed his friends back in Philippi. He was worried about their well-being because they were intimidated by what they saw in their society. They risked losing their church because of the division among believers. Paul felt that the effort he had put into starting the church would be lost entirely.

He and Timothy wrote a letter to the Philippians; Epaphroditus delivered it and read it to the believers out loud. This was a lesson plan from Paul. He gave these intimidated people a curriculum for thinking differently when everything seemed lost. It's a letter for us, too, when we are going through a time of grief and loss over injustice, a job loss, or a life transition. This letter is a lesson plan for losers. Paul begins with three foundational ideas that will guide the lesson.

Watch Out for the Haters

First, Paul warns us not to get caught up with the "haters," whom he refers to as "dogs" who always try to draw us into a fight (Philippians 3:2-4, 18-19). They are the first-century version of cancel culture. These dogs are divisive and have their own issues to deal with. My older son Parker's kindergarten teacher advised his class, "Ignore bad behavior." In the same way, Paul and Timothy advised us not to get drawn into intimidating battles that only wound us further and do nothing to resolve conflicts.

Flush the Accomplishments

Second, Paul tells us to treat our achievements as poop (Phil 3:8). In Greek, that word is *skubala*. And yes, as far as I know, this is a curse word. Paul wants us to flush the titles, promotions, and wins down the drain. Like Jesus, he wants us to know that our success is not found in what we *do* but in who we *are*. That means many of the ribbons and trophies have to go. I threw away a lot of old plaques that reinforced my identity as someone who was "successful." I saved many of the mementos that reminded me of people who made a difference in my life.

Focus on Jesus

Third, Paul says to focus on Jesus's suffering and resurrection (Phil 3:10-11). Just as Jesus gave his disciples a vision on the Mt. of Transfiguration, so Paul and Timothy describe a similar focus from prison. In Paul's day at the Olympics, the tape at the end was called the "scopos," similar to our word for the scope of a rifle or telescope. Paul and Timothy ask "What are you focused on through your scope?" If your goal is personal achievement and ambition, you are setting yourself up for an empty life. Make your goal to bear witness to the reign of Christ in the resurrection. Develop a greater knowledge of Jesus's life and ministry. Let his death and resurrection guide your decision-making.

Track Your Progress

Paul urges us to think carefully and start tracking how we journey toward a life of joy. The goal is to rejoice in the Lord always (Phil 4:4). How do we stay joyful even when life is falling apart and the dogs are hounding us? This discipline requires more than taking long walks to cool down. He echoes a process that Cicero taught: focused thinking on the good so that we become more accustomed to suffering and can learn from it. "There is great power in virtues; rouse them if the chance to droop." [Young, LCL] Then Cicero goes onto explain four virtues that if practiced will cause a person to forget about their misfortunes: fortitude, temperance, justice, and prudence.[2]

Paul wants us to treat life as if we were preparing for a test—making lists, tracking our progress, and giving ourselves a grade on a list of eight virtues that are similar to Cicero's. Paul wants us to "account for these things"[3] in our lives in light of his previous focus on Jesus (Phil 4:8). If we're not going to track achievements, grades, or our future plans, then what can we think about most of the time to have a joyful and wise life?

Paul and Timothy's eight virtues are the characteristics of a life lived joyfully. Your identity is in Jesus, and if you are willing to lose the life you thought you were going to have, what then will be at your core? These eight virtues provide a mental roadmap for assessing our priorities. The roadmap helps us decide which books we read, which projects to undertake, which organizations we join, and even which people to date or befriend. They are like stretching exercises or practice lessons for becoming better at losership. They are a scope to evaluate whether your day is successful based on your identity in Jesus. They work together collectively; no single concept works in isolation from the others.[4]

We might be tempted to think this is a staircase of self-help success, but each step isn't an accomplishment to achieve; it's a gift to receive. Our operating systems are infected with the achievement virus, so we shouldn't expect to get an "A" on the exam. God already sees these qualities in us. God treats us as saints and calls us holy people. Jesus has already done the work on us that needs to be done.

Here's another surprise: these aren't exclusively Christian virtues. Remember Cicero believes in living virtuously! We can find these traits in many people we encounter. Paul and Timothy did, and Jesus did, too. We don't need to be Christians to live this way. But because you are a Christian, you will utilize these characteristics in a way that centers Christ. Jesus is like a key that unlocks these doors and allows you to live differently. If you take a philosophy course in college, you might want to have these virtues handy. You can learn from philosophy; in Paul's case, he learned from the Stoics and Jews and incorporated their teachings into this list. When people saw the list, they could see what made the virtues distinctively Christian.

As we actively think through and track these eight concepts while graduating from high school and moving into college, we can sift through our decisions, avoid snap judgments, and redirect our intentions toward Jesus.[5] Taking these steps will allow us to grieve well when we lose what we love. When we are treated unfairly and unjustly, we can turn to this list to help us sort things out.[6]

None of us are experts in these eight qualities. Imagine you are a toddler trying to climb your first set of stairs. Your parents or other caregivers might actually remember this. They observed you to ensure you were well guarded and protected. (I clearly remember the first time my son Drake *fell* down the stairs.) Each step led to another. Sometimes, you started over from the bottom and worked your way up crawling. When you reached the top, you turned to see who was watching you. We have a need and desire to be seen. It doesn't count unless someone notices. Beginners have no problem falling because they know they have much to learn. The word "disciple" means "learner," and we need to have the mindset of a novice when practicing our walk with Jesus.

The Loser's Staircase

Are you ready to take the steps? Here are the eight concepts in Philippians 4:8:

> Finally, brothers and sisters, whatever is true, whatever is honorable, whatever is just, whatever is holy, whatever is pleasurable, whatever is reputable—if anything is virtuous or praiseworthy—think about such things. (My translation)

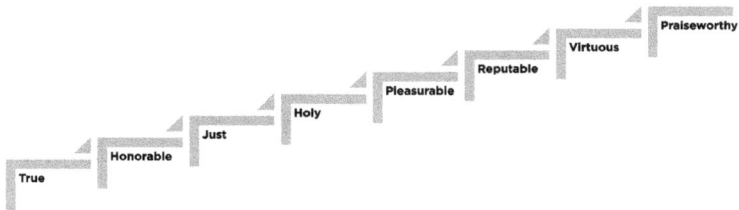

Whatever is *true* means honest, genuine, real, authentic. Paul and Timothy invite their readers to account for a life lived truthfully and vulnerably—not report their adherence to a list of facts or statements that are "the truth." More important to a joyful life is whether the way you live when you are alone is the same way you live when you are with others. School teaches us to memorize and pursue "the truth" or abstract concepts, but there is no truth without a person who lives it and a community around you to walk with you. How you live says more about what you believe than anything you say or post on social media.

We also reflect on what we know to be true when we fail. Everyone needs something to hold on to when life bottoms out. Reflect and live into what you know to be true and trustworthy. Express gratitude for and to the people who help you remember, which leads us naturally to the next step.[7]

To think *honorably* means to behave in a way that causes people to respect you (1 Tim 3:8-11; Titus 2:2). Character and advice are interrelated. Honorable means that you live above reproach, and your words are trustworthy.[8] Listen to trustworthy people who give reliable advice.

The word *just* also means equitable. This was a hot topic in Paul and Timothy's day and still is in ours. Justice was one of the four cardinal virtues of the ancient world. They were the *cardo* (from the Latin word for hinge on a door) or hinges to open a door and direct a person's life. Many campuses, workplaces, and investment portfolios focus on a secular definition of diversity, equity, and inclusion (DEI). But what do Christians think about these things?

Equity or justice is at the heart of the biblical message but is rarely discussed as something to think about. Paul and Timothy want us to consider and account for biblical justice where we live—the equitable, humane, and just treatment of others. Life is unfair, and we can't right every wrong that has occurred to other people. But we cannot live in isolation from others while those outside the church remain oppressed or are victims of injustice. We are bound together in a covenant citizenship of justice. Ironically, by learning to lose ourselves, we can empathize with those who are oppressed, listen to their grievances, and decide how to respond. Usually, those responses do not require a Facebook post or generate publicity. They involve the quiet, behind-the-scenes work of believers who help and advocate for people left behind.

There are two ways to think about responses to injustice ahead of time: personal and systemic. Personal ways are the primary ways that you already reach out to those who are lonely. When people are sitting alone, you make sure they have a friend beside them. When anti-Semitic hate is on the rise, you reach out to Jewish friends and express your concern for them. When police wound Black men, check on your Black friends. These are simple ways to show you care.

The second way is the systemic way. If you are in a position of influence where you can speak up, then do so. Check policies, and admit your blind spots. Taking a stand might cost you a job or a level of influence within your organization. Because you have already decided to surrender the life you thought you had, you are well positioned to stand up for others and ensure your organization, company, church, and club are doing what is just and right.

The next step is to think about what is *pure* or *holy*, meaning that we recognize that God treats us as holy people. According to Paul and Timothy, we are already saints in God's eyes. Because you trust in God, you can do nothing to become any purer. No doubt you have done things that make you feel ashamed; you have prayed, confessed your sins, and have sought to make things right. Being holy or pure does not mean carrying the weight of shame from past mistakes with us for the rest of our lives. Paul urges us instead to focus on the sincere motives (Phil 1:17) we are to have with each other and on treating each other as saints.

If we are already holy people, what does it mean to treat others in the church as saints? It means seeing other people the way God sees them and treating them accordingly. It means living out of that holiness together as you go about your different, separate lives around people on your campus and in your city. There should be something noticeably different about your behavior, motives, and decisions because God has already made you holy.

Step 5 is fascinating because it takes us out of the New Testament world and into Paul and Timothy's Roman world. The word *pleasurable* or *delightful* puts a smile on my face. Paul integrates what people normally thought of in his day into biblical teaching. We can't find the word he uses here anywhere else in the New Testament, but the concept appears often in Greek and Roman literature, philosophy, and speeches. I have experienced it in hanging around my small group for seven years. They are a delight and a true pleasure to be around, making others want to hang out with them. They enjoy one another's company, bring energy, and make others feel better.[9] We should be the kind of people and community who are endearing to others.[10] Make your gatherings a delight, full of laughter, play, and celebration. People should feel better after being with you and other Christ followers.[11]

The next step reiterates the previous one and emphasizes why we should be so fun and enjoyable. Paul says to think on what is *reputable* (2 Cor 6:8).[12] We should be so highly regarded that people share good reports about us and want to be around us.[13] In other words, there should be a winsome quality to our work, study, and family life.

We are almost at the top of the stairs; the last two are the summit. Something *virtuous* is anything of high moral character deemed praiseworthy by others and God. This is the only time we find the word *virtuous* in the Pauline corpus, and its significance here cannot be overstated.[14]

These are the virtues to which we should aspire. By doing so, we will receive praise from God and others. Rhetorically, the phrase "virtuous and praiseworthy" moves the Philippians to the summit of their thinking. We turn around now to hear and see the applause of others and, most importantly, God. This is the high-five moment of our lives—the peak joy.

Our actions inspire others, and we call back to them from the top of the stairs—"Climb up! This is an absolute thrill!"

Thinking first rather than reacting in snap judgment allows us to own our behavior and redirect our intentions toward Christ. Paul and Timothy provide a stairway for the mind to consider on the journey to joy. At the summit, we look around and realize our minds are in the right spot. How do we keep going? We need a group around us that looks something like a loser's circle.

Discussion Questions

1. The loser journey doesn't require expertise, just willingness to think like a toddler exploring. When have you tried to learn something new? What did that feel like?

2. Paul was isolated and in prison when he and Timothy decided to write about the "loser staircase." A place of loneliness can be the beginning of a new mindset. When have you been isolated but sensed God's presence?

3. Take a look at the eight steps on the staircase. Which one is your strongest virtue? Where do you need help?

Chapter 6

The Loser's Circle

Most stadiums in America have a "circle of honor," a "hall of fame," or a particular group that became famous because of their accomplishments. Christian fame and honor are different. If you have not figured it out by now, our group is more like the "fellowship of the ring" from the *Lord of the Rings* or the children in *The Chronicles of Narnia*. We are scared, afraid, and unqualified, and we make mistakes. We also need to surround ourselves with essential people on the journey.

Losing takes more than a vision, a class, and a different way of thinking. We need to trust some people with our story and invite them to pour into us in significant ways. Paul and Timothy did that for each other, and so did the team accompanying them on the journey—women and men such as Phoebe, Priscilla, Aquila, Lydia, Apollos, and many more who came in and out of their circle but were openly and vulnerably linked together. They did five things for each other, listed in Philippians 4:9: "Whatever you have learned or received or heard from me, or seen in me—put it into practice. And the God of peace will be with you."

They learned, received, heard, saw, and practiced. They treated this like a naturalization process for a new citizen of their country. They considered themselves migrants from heaven colonizing Earth, and this is how they would continue to model and demonstrate the process of losership going forward. We could draw the process like the diagram below.

By thinking of it as a cycle, we will feel God's peace and experience the joy of living that we have discussed throughout this book.

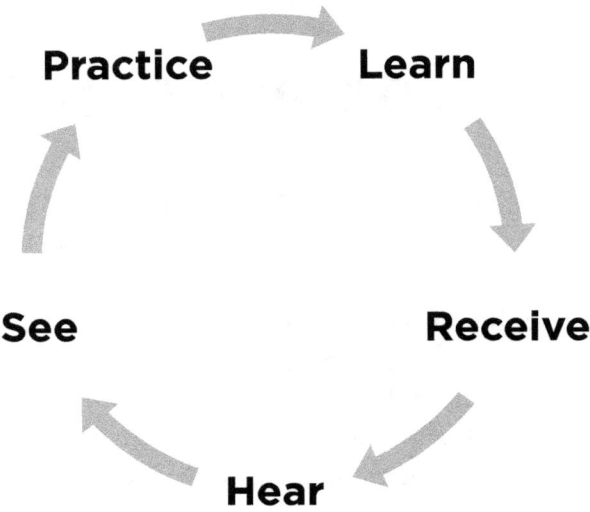

We all need people like Paul and Timothy in our lives. They do not have to be experts but can serve as a "personal board of spiritual directors" for a joyful life. We invite them to continue to pour into us. We also need at least one other person outside our immediate families who can observe our lives and behaviors. These people might emerge as we share our stories with them. They might give us an assignment or a place to serve that allows us to go deeper into the joyful discovery of the life that Jesus wants us to have.

What do you do in this loser's circle? You track the staircase virtues using five essential methods. First, *learn* everything you can from each other. You are already familiar with this process from school and likely from church. Never stop learning and acquiring information.[1] Paul and Timothy offer authoritative instructions as spiritual parents to the Philippian siblings (3:17-19; 4:1-3; see also 2 Tim 2:1-3).[2] Every person needs spiritual parents and grandparents who can share Jesus's teachings, allow you to emulate them, connect you to other losers in your community, and help you form your identity around Jesus's call to lose your life to save it. Some people are fortunate to have these kinds of people in their immediate families or church families.[3]

Most people need someone outside their immediate circle "on the bridge." Sociologists call them our social capital bridge friends. They are not the people we usually bond with. They are people we admire and see occasionally, and they have experienced a loss that Jesus has transformed or used in some way. Ideally, these are two people—not just one—so they can hold you and themselves accountable. Jesus sent out disciples in pairs for a reason. You invite these people to be your spiritual parents and grandparents on the journey of faith.

You must receive and adopt your teachers' instructions in the next phase. Paul and Timothy indicate that they *received* education from others. They did not invent these teachings. People taught them, and then they passed these ideas along to others. This model was popular among rabbis and in oral performances to a group, where it resembled delivering a speech to an audience.[4]

The third method is to listen or *hear*; in the Greek world, it was also rendered "read."[5] In ancient times, the words "hear" and "read" were often interchangeable. If a copy of a book was available, someone read the book aloud to a group. Most people listened to books being read to them the way we listen to a podcast or audiobook.[6] Reading and listening are the key to learning, receiving, seeing, and practicing.[7] By reading together, we bind ourselves to our bridge friends and the cloud of witnesses cheering us forward. By listening to someone's works read aloud and applying them, listeners can imitate an absentee moral figure. In this case, reading and listening to the Bible aloud brings the characters from the past into the present for us to imagine how they might live if faced with our circumstances, classes, and communities. This leads us to the next step in the cycle.

Step 4 is *seeing*. The Philippians have heard Paul, Timothy, and so many other figures and the ways they succeeded and failed. Learning involves seeing or visualizing how you and your teachers will carry out the learning process in your world. You visualize your day, your month, your year, knowing you have examples to reflect on like a mirror. These examples become an inspiration to you and sow seeds into your heart that later yield fruit.[8] Invite your teachers to help you track how you are living out the eight virtues of losership, reflect each day on your progress, and continue to walk through the door of surrender.

In the process, you will learn what to *practice*. Let's return to the idea of thinking like a beginner. Paul and Timothy encourage us to practice our faith as we might learn to play an instrument for the first time or start a sport. Faith is not an adjective describing our lives, and it's not a noun to name something we get as a result of being a Christian. Faith is doing. By living according to our beliefs, we show faith. Sometimes that feels like uncertainty, insecurity, and doubt, but by practicing, we are "faithing."[9]

Practice the way a surgeon works in the operating room or a pilot flies a plane. They start with a checklist and do a "dry run" before attempting the real thing. They go into the process knowing there will be challenges along the way. But they and their team are ready and prepared to improvise.[10]

In my field of preaching, I learned that the sermons that connected best with the audience did not follow a script but instead adapted to the room. I prepared, planned, and rehearsed, but I was open to the unexpected person who arrived or the unplanned moment. Some of these people were Hurricane Katrina survivors. The unplanned moments were related to gun violence: a shooting at a nearby Unitarian church, Sandy Hook Elementary, Mother Emmanuel Church, or the Florida State campus library. At a conference following COVID, I had to respond extemporaneously to a hate-filled diatribe from a contemporary "Christian" artist. Life is full of unexpected hate and vengeance. I needed to adapt along the way and trust the unexpected that the Spirit would give me the words to say in the moment..

To help you along the way, I have provided a starter tracker system for you to use with your teachers. Paul and Timothy do not ask us to do anything they have not already attempted. Your teachers should do these steps with you and, ideally, invite a couple of friends to join you. Expect that failure will be a part of the process. That's the joy of the journey.

The effect of this process is God's peace remaining with "y'all." This word is how I know Paul and Timothy were Southerners—the "you" in Philippians 4:10 is plural. God's peace is like a guardian protecting us through the difficulties of loss and failure. Collectively, we receive peace that repairs relationships in our communities and calms us in the face of adversity.

A Place to Begin

How does a loser's circle begin? Not everyone is ready or qualified to join. I've learned in my journey that you meet at least three kinds of friends: service friends, struggler friends, and soul friends. Service friends know you because of your identity as a president, pastor, or fundraiser. You rarely hear from them because they no longer need your services. After I left Northern, I was disappointed not to hear from more people I had helped in ministry service. We shared so many conferences, meetings, and memories together around church work. My expectations were wrong about their role in my life.

Through God's grace, I met two other kinds of friends who are perfect for a loser's circle. Struggler friends who have also failed will reach out to encourage me. A small, tight circle of soul friends check in with me, show up, call, and stay in touch. They are good listeners, assertive, and direct. I have compiled a list of helpful things they have said to me that may help you or someone you know who is experiencing vocational loss or uncertainty. Each statement is specific or open-ended.

"I know you as someone kind, gracious, and caring. That's my experience with you."

"You are in my prayers today, and I am specifically praying for _____."

"You did really good work at _____, and I wanted you to know that I saw what you accomplished and will remember that."

"This Bible verse came to mind, and I wanted to share it with you."

"I am coming to see you, and a good time for me is the month of _____. What's your schedule that month?"

"How is your family holding up, and how can I be praying for them?"

"There was a time in my life when I had to work on this issue, and here's what I did."

"Tell me about your time at _____. It must have been so difficult. What are some of the good times you had?"

"This must be so hard. What happened is not right, and I'm here to listen."

Avoid glib text messages that say, "I'm praying for you" or "How are you?" When I've answered those questions, rarely has anyone responded. Check in with people. The moment you think of the other person, that is the time they need to hear from you. And don't leave them hanging.

A loser's circle provides a network for talking through your experiences. What if you do not have a group of spiritual parents and grandparents? An excellent place to start is an assisted living center or nursing home or with a Christian mentor suffering from a terminal illness. Do you remember my story about "Pastor David" in the nursing home? He understood the power of sitting with and ministering to dying people. They are not problems to solve; they are mysteries to embrace and receive. By being with people, we confront our fears of death. We cannot look away, so we must pay attention to what matters—practicing presence with the person.[11] We open up to allow them to share their wisdom with us, and then we start practicing what they tell us.

Four years ago, one of my fellow swim parents was diagnosed with ALS, also known as Lou Gehrig's disease. He invited me into a unique form of the "loser's circle," a regular card game of euchre. I had to learn to play the game (to think like a beginner), and now I enjoy visiting with him twice a month. He has taught me so much about facing death. He shares his testimony openly, gives Bibles to athletes worldwide, and faces death and decay courageously. He never wanted to experience this, and all of us would do anything possible to take the disease away from him. But we have learned from him how to welcome and embrace loss. He radiates joy.

Discussion Questions

1. Think about the friends you hang out with the most. Are they service friends, strugglers, or soul friends? Who do you need to spend more time with?

2. Who are your spiritual parents and grandparents? What have they already poured into you? Who could you ask to be a part of this journey with you?

3. Who are the people you could pour into?

4. What areas of your journey would you like to start practicing?

5. Who do you want to learn from?

6. What traditions or teachings have you received?

7. What do you want to read or listen to?

8. What do you want to emulate that you'd like to see in others?

Chapter 7

Characteristics of Joy

Although you have not seen him, you love him; and even though you do not see him now, you believe in him and rejoice with an indescribable and glorious joy. (1 Peter 1:8)

Throughout this book, we have discussed the doorway or portal to a joyful life. But we need to know what kind of life this is. If we walk through the portal into a life of joy, what can we expect to find?

God is already proud of us, and God's joy grows as we complete God's assignments. God wants us to learn and grow in this work. God does not expect perfection but plans for risks and failures on our part. Remember, God has multiple plans, and all of them are for our best. God is going to work with our mistakes. If God can work with disciples unable to heal a demon-possessed boy, a disciple who denied Christ, and one who betrayed Christ, God can work with us.

The joy you find in a life with God cannot be contained within yourself; you must share it with others. We do not operate in silos; we share our experiences with other people and are a part of their experiences. That's why the work students do to be at church, bring their friends, and keep coming to church inspires me. That is joyful work. The church is not merely a place to go that sends you out to do the work of service in the world. Attending, inviting, worshiping, and sharing life as the church on Sundays and throughout the week is the work. I will share six characteristics that contribute to this joy. You will begin to experience it slowly as you walk forward on your journey with Christ.

Obedient

Joy comes from an *obedient* lifestyle. This is a decision on our part, many times against the odds of the circumstances we face. We must decide if we want to go through the doorway into this lifestyle. Mary exalted in God's decision to choose her joyfully, but not without thought, reflection, and support from her relative, Elizabeth. She built a file system in her mind and a memory bank of things from her past to draw from in the future. She "kept all these things and pondered them in her heart." Her joy came from the deep place of a heart filled with assuring memories. She chose joy in a situation that could have been bleak.

Adventurous

Joy is an *adventurous* ride full of laughter and play. Did I mention that joy is a lot of fun? Beyond the happiness that comes from a momentary thrill or a pay raise, God's joy causes deep belly laughs even when we see our frailties and helplessness. We learn to accept our faults and trust that God will use them. This joy responds to God's actions with a raucous celebration of noise, music, disruption, and surprises. This joy does not need a strategy; it thrives on chaos and spontaneity.

We are on a journey together like the Israelites leaving Egypt heading to the promised land. College and post-college work and life are a wilderness time full of snakes, doubt, and uncertainty. God's presence is more cloud-like and unsettled. All of this is actually a sign that you are headed in the right direction. Do not worry about settling down, planting roots, changing majors, or making long-term decisions. Instead, lean into the presence of God with you and the people of God around you. Keep moving on the journey, and trust that the journey is the destination.[1]

Endurance

Joy provides *endurance* to continue through the next challenge you face. Today's popular word is "resilience," but the New Testament does not know much about that. We are often broken, afraid, and alone. When we put the pieces back together, we are converted and resurrected—but rarely do we bounce back the way we were. This joy means persistence and flexibility. We are working through the difficulties and developing confidence that good can come out of bad situations. When we come out of a struggle, we are wiser and more enlightened, compassionate, and confident. We go beyond resilience into growth and transformation.[2]

Attentive

Joy requires *attentive* listening to God's words through Scripture. One example is the eunuch in Acts 8:26-40. He may not have understood what he was reading, but he was paying attention, reading the book of Isaiah aloud, and trusting that God would reveal the meaning to him as he went along the journey. He exemplifies someone whose journey through loss led him to joy. While he reads the book aloud, the deacon Philip mysteriously arrives. We know the Spirit transported him, and Philip responds to what he hears from the Scripture reading and asks the eunuch, "Do you know what you are reading?" They work together through Isaiah, informing each other's interpretations. In response, Philip baptizes the eunuch. When the Spirit whisks Philip away, the eunuch goes "on his way rejoicing." This joy in the journey would not be possible without the eunuch first being willing to listen attentively to God's words.

Prayerful

Joy is a *prayerful* conversation between you and God and with you and others to God. Remember, you are joining a discussion God already has with you through Scripture, nature, and the people around you. You do not have to initiate the conversation. God is talking to us already. Interruptions are frequent and welcome. I have met the best role models for this process in Chicago through preaching and serving with historically Black churches. In these services, Christians are already joining God's vibrant conversations through call, response, quiet reflection, and exuberant praise.

Quietly Confident

Joy is *quietly confident*. As 1 Peter 1:18 says, God's kind of joy is unspeakable, as if reflecting on a vision of Jesus that we have not found the words to express. This is the kind of joy parents have when their children are baptized. For many people, an early baptism is imparted on them. Later, they decide to make their own choices, and eventually their faith becomes their own. For others, baptism is a personal choice made after a commitment to Jesus. All of us have a continual decision to make to express our dedication and commitment to God. We do that through a "joy unspeakable," a quiet reflection that reminds us of our commitments, the baptism experience, and the new era moving forward.[3]

Discussion Questions

1. Joy is often considered an energetic emotion, but the Bible speaks of several dimensions to joy: a decision, space, promise, and quiet confidence. What kind of joy have you experienced?

2. Read Acts 8:26-40. Listening to Scripture was an essential step that led the eunuch to discover joy. What are some of the steps he took that you could take today?

Return to Joy

Think about death or, instead, if you prefer, migration to heaven. It is a beautiful thing to learn to die. (Seneca, *Epistles* 26.9)

I will prepare a place for you, and if I go and prepare a place for you, I will come again and receive you unto myself. (Jesus, John 14:2-3)

Keep death daily before one's eyes. (Rule of St. Benedict 4.47)

In light of the six characteristics of Christian joy, how do we arrive at this destination? Once again, we look to the early believers as examples. They did not set out to find joy. They received joy because of their outlook on life. They were animated by the sense that Jesus would return to earth at any moment. They were excited about his return and unconcerned about their death. They had faced the fact that they would not be able to solve every problem; their lives would be full of failure and loss, but one day, Jesus would come back to set things right again.

It seems strange to mention the end of life in a book for people about to graduate from high school. Here we are in this liminal space, ready to send you off on a grand adventure, yet we remind you of the end of time and our ultimate ending of death. But that is precisely what it means to practice losership and find joy in life. When we know and realize that Jesus will return, and one day we will die and be in his presence, that promise becomes a powerful force in our lives to share with the world.

My late theology professor, A. J. Conyers, wrote,

> For early Christians, the ultimate destiny of the world had already been staked out. They knew where the world was going because they remembered it; they had already seen it. The fact that God would prevail and that the best efforts of evil to overcome would fail was no longer in question.[1]

These early believers remembered what they saw and experienced in Jesus's suffering, death, and resurrection. They sang about it in Philippians 2:6-11 and realized that this pattern was a forecast of the future. They remembered what the future would be like and knew that in the end there would be joy. We don't know what will happen in the future, nor do we try to control the future, but we do know who will be with us in the future—God.

My hope is that you will not wait until the end to experience joy, but will welcome the crisis and the gift it gives you. This is what it means to lose your life *for the sake of the gospel*. The gospel introduces a crisis that turns our lives away from what would kill us into a world of sacrifice, service, and joy that will save us. The apocalyptic moments that pull back the curtain on our times today reveal the need to trust in God and show how helpless our world is to fix and save itself. We are forced and confronted with a life-giving decision. We can change, accept the lessons from failure, or stay the same, returning to the path we were on. Either way, we must decide.

Hubris or pride is the refusal to become humble by what should have humiliated us.[2] Receive the gift that Jesus offers you now, surrender the life you thought you would have, and experience what Jesus invites you to do.

We do not convert, change, or learn loss and surrender through reprimand and punishment. I grew up hearing a kind of legalistic, fear-based preaching at my Christian school and transferred much of that philosophy into my early parenting. I assumed everything would be fine if we could set the proper boundaries, build the correct foundation, and provide the appropriate guard rails. Little did I know that this process began a discovery. The way to grow as parents and people is through loss, failure, and suffering. There is no other path to joy.

My philosophy is much different now, and I share some of it in this book. I developed something I first read about from the Apostle Paul: rejoicing and prayer. Instead of revisiting the past, we are to respond to God's inbreaking work from the future. We are to look ahead. Theologian Jürgen Moltmann wrote, "We do not change through imperatives to be new and to change. Repentance is a return to the future."[3]

We discovered in chapter 5 that repentance means changing our minds. Doing so means tracking our progress much differently as willing losers. We turn our minds to the idea that Jesus is on the way and breaking into our world even now. He's the fixer, not us. His transfiguration is the picture, and his parables provide the script and announce the arrival of his work in the world right now.

Repentance, understood in the old way, returns us to the evil and our past. Fear-based repentance deals in self-accusation, contrition, anger, and ashes. But a joyful repentance, which we describe here, "looks to the future rejoicing in new self-confidence and love."[4] We mourn wrongs that occur, but we do so with the desire to heal and relate to one another as

Christian citizens for the sake of the other person, the sake of the community, and the sake of the larger world.

What does that mean for you? Allow Jesus to tell you a story from Matthew 25:14-30.

Share in the Joy

(14) For it is as if a man, going on a journey, summoned his slaves and entrusted his property to them; (15) to one he gave five talents, to another two, to another one, to each according to his ability. Then he went away. (16) The one who had received the five talents went off at once and traded with them, and made five more talents. (17) In the same way, the one who had the two talents made two more talents. (18) But the one who had received the one talent went off and dug a hole in the ground and hid his master's money. (19) After a long time the master of those slaves came and settled accounts with them. (20) Then the one who had received the five talents came forward, bringing five more talents, saying, "Master, you handed over to me five talents; see, I have made five more talents." (21) His master said to him, "Well done, good and trustworthy slave; you have been trustworthy in a few things, I will put you in charge of many things; enter into the joy of your master." (22) And the one with the two talents also came forward, saying, "Master, you handed over to me two talents; see, I have made two more talents." (23) His master said to him, "Well done, good and trustworthy slave; you have been trustworthy in a few things, I will put you in charge of many things; enter into the joy of your master." (24) Then the one who had received the one talent also came forward, saying, "Master, I knew that you were a harsh man, reaping where you did not sow, and gathering where you did not scatter seed; (25) so I was afraid, and I went and hid your talent in the ground. Here you have what is yours." (26) But his

master replied, "You wicked and lazy slave! You knew, did you, that I reap where I did not sow, and gather where I did not scatter? (27) Then you ought to have invested my money with the bankers, and on my return I would have received what was my own with interest. (28) So take the talent from him, and give it to the one with the ten talents. (29) For to all those who have, more will be given, and they will have an abundance; but from those who have nothing, even what they have will be taken away. (30) As for this worthless slave, throw him into the outer darkness, where there will be weeping and gnashing of teeth." (Matthew 25:14-30 NRSV)

In our church, we hear a lot about the parable of the sheep and the goats. We are encouraged that whatever we have done "for the least of these," we have done for Jesus. I love that parable about the end of time, but the one that precedes it is even better. This parable is what I call the pathway into a joyful life that does the things described in Matthew 25:31-46. The one in verses 14-30 paints a picture of the times we live, the people we are around today, and the posture we will take toward the future.

Joseph and Pharaoh

In Jesus's parable, the enslaved characters' experiences in Matthew 25:15 are analagous to Joseph's life in Genesis 37-50. The book of Genesis describes how Joseph suffered injustice—twice! First, his brothers sold him into slavery, and during his enslavement, he was accused of illicit behavior with the wife of the Egyptian official Potiphar and imprisoned for it. Joseph is the poster boy for losership in the Old Testament. He was not, of course, without flaws, and he had an ego issue. Yet he remained as faithful as possible, and Pharaoh entrusted him with vital power and possessions as a part of the court. Joseph was the one, as Jesus described, who was tasked with a few things and eventually put in charge of many things. He ultimately used those possessions to bless the people who once sold him into slavery. None of us would describe Joseph's life as joyful unless we had a different definition. After reuniting with his family, Joseph offered the true mark of someone who has mastered losership. He told them, "what you intended for harm, God intended for good, that is the saving of many lives" (Genesis 50:20). That is a true joy.

Jesus said we are now the Josephs who have lost and failed and learned to live with different priorities. The plans we have are no longer the plan. The disastrous situation of being sold into slavery and then living life downward is now our assignment in life. God may not have intended it this way, but God will use this assignment to help others.

If you learn nothing else from this book, please learn this: make plans, visions, dreams, strategies, and goals out of the surprises that happen—the things you did not plan for. When disaster strikes or problems come, you will know what to do and say because you have taken the steps of the faith journey.

Jesus said in Luke 21:15 that difficult things would happen. So continually ground yourself in the new mindset we discussed in chapter 4, and surround yourself with people who can help you process these issues, think through them, and determine your assignment.

Respond to Crises

When I was a pastor, I thought my job was to "come up with a vision," share it with the congregation, build a team, and move forward together. I never really had that luxury. Most places I served had issues and problems I inherited, and I had to respond to needs rather than develop new opportunities to serve. When we were ready to start new things, another wave of challenges hit. This was certainly the case in Knoxville, Tennessee. We had wave after wave of challenges with resources, debt, and staff transitions. But God seemed most present with us in disaster. When Hurricane Katrina struck, the waves of water washed evacuees ashore in Knoxville. Former Vice President Al Gore flew about sixty people out of the New Orleans Superdome and landed in east Tennessee, his home state. They were transported to Baptist Hospital across the river from our church on Labor Day weekend. One of our church members who had experience with the Red Cross and caring for refugees in Burundi reached out to offer our church gym as a temporary shelter to house those released from the hospital. Pastor Jud Reasons assembled a rapid response team, and the evacuees arrived that weekend. I left a UT home football game to help set up the gym and prepare for our guests. They were only with us for a week, but that week gave me a glimpse of the future. We mobilized everyone to clean bathrooms, serve our guests, and be the church in the building. We had a lot of joy serving together, and that process led us to create a new position on our staff to serve the local community's needs as much as our guests' needs.

As Rebecca Solnit writes, in disaster a community emerges that institutions, governments, and organizations cannot imitate. Human bonds form in a crisis that reveals who we are and shows us the way forward. Be prepared and ready for this opportunity and the people who emerge from the experience.[5]

This is a picture of the opportunities God is giving us now—the unplanned assignments. Jesus, our Master, waits to see what we will do with what he has given us. The easy solution, and the most prevalent in our society, is the one we have warned you about—to try to save your life. This idea is based on a false notion that God is hard and difficult, mean and regimented. That God has high standards, and we will never live up to them. There's not a lot of smiling here—just fear. The "dogs" Paul mentions in Philippians have no reason to enjoy life because they are afraid of God or of losing their influence. Many of us think the best we can do is try to hang on to what we have, build our reputations, enlarge our influence, and take our fear, anger, and guilt out on others. Ultimately, we vote ourselves out of the party and send ourselves into the outer darkness to remain in fear.

But believers have seen a different view of God lived out in Jesus and in our church. God is actually kind, loving, joyful, and fun to be around. God cares deeply for us and wants the best for us. God has already made us his saints and invites us on a journey involving risk, uncertainty, loose plans, and laughter.

This is the life of losership. In our community, we understand that the Master will return, and some people would say current events in our world only confirm how close that time is. I will leave that for another book. What I will tell you is that conflicts, loss, death, and war only awaken us to the reality that we need Jesus to return. While he waits, he has an assignment. He wants us to—you guessed it—try to lose it all. He wants us to take what he's given us and risk those possessions and blessings on the very people and projects that are his priorities—the least, the last, the lost, the left out. Behind the scenes, he wants us to visit hurting people, care for migrants, look after each other, clothe the naked, and give cups of cold water to orphans and widows.

How do we choose what to do? With the help of your "loser's circle," I would suggest picking something that comes out of the pain and suffering you have experienced. The lessons you have learned are now the inspiration you need to help others. You know better how to care for people because you have been through something that they have experienced.

One of your college majors or first jobs might be something that helps you process the pain and loss you grieve. Bruce Feiler calls this motivation your "toothache," the problem in your life that shaped you so much that it becomes the catalyst for your calling. For me, the death of my dad and my pastor's visit afterward shaped my imagination about what people need when they lose parents—someone to show up, pray, and let a child cry on a brown tie. I still remember that visit vividly. What you lose can become your toothache that nags you until you discover a way to help our world move forward with similar losses.

Even if you do not volunteer or work in your "toothache" area, you will learn to empathize better with others who are going through failure, loss, and weakness. People are often uncomfortable around those who are dealing with loss. It is rare for someone caring to reach out and repeatedly ask how a person is doing. People want you to see them and know their problems. Bring up the issue that caused the failure. The hurting person hurts as much in silence as they do when discussing the subject. Tell them the good qualities you see in them. If they have lost a child or loved one, or if their child is in a treatment center, share stories about the loved one. These stories are a healing balm. They need to remember the good times and know that others also recognize them. The time and place when you think to reach out are always the right time and place for the person who needs you.

As we go, God will inspect our efforts and tell us, "Well done, good and faithful servant; come share in the joy of the Master." We are invited to share *God's* joy. That's not a personal feeling but a joyful space where God's presence is our guide, where we are in God's territory, and where there is abundant goodwill for all. By God's grace, we can do what

Joseph did—save the lives of those who have treated us unfairly and unjustly.

Instead of hoarding our gifts, God wants us to use them to help others. The signal of God's pride in us that we will get more work to do. We will receive another assignment, tasked with risking God's investment in us to serve other people. We might get a few more times to rise and fall and learn to fail repeatedly. This is a sign that we're in the loser's circle and on our way to joy.

Discussion Questions

1. Does Jesus's return evoke fear or excitement for you? How do you react when you hear about the promise of his coming?

2. Instead of planning for the future, Jesus wants us to be prepared for whatever crisis the future brings. What problem in the world are you burdened for? What could God be calling you to respond to?

3. Joseph faced two kinds of injustice and lived long enough to repay his persecutors kindly. What injustice have you faced in your life? Have you been able to be generous or show mercy in these experiences?

Chapter Summaries for Group Discussions

Chapter 1: The "Life 360" Plans I Have for You

Summary: Achievement Christianity is a virus that equates Jesus' blessings and vision for life as material benefits, educational excellence, and personal authority and power. The idea is based on a false interpretation of Jeremiah 29:11, that God has a personalized success plan for your life.

Symptoms of the Achievement Virus

Half-truths
Sadness
Material Blessings
Platitudes
Comparison
Anger and Rage
Control
Surveillance
Boredom and Escape
Stuck and Drifting

Discussion Questions

1. What is "achievement Christianity," and where do you see it today?

2. Why is "achievement Christianity" like a virus? What does it do to us?

3. Have you seen or experienced any of these symptoms?

4. Read the story of Eutychus in Acts 20:7-12. How is he similar to the biblical character Jonah?

Chapter 2: Lose Your Life

Summary: Joyful people have gone through a season of life where they have lost something either through misfortune, mistakes, or unjust hardships. Jesus doesn't treat suffering as a sign of failure. Jesus explains that suffering is a part of life. He offers a vision for us to follow. If we are willing to surrender the parts of our lives that desire to achieve more, we can experience true joy and salvation.

Read Mark 8:31–9:29.

Discussion Questions

1. Reflect on the transfiguration scene. How did this event change the disciples' vision of Jesus' ministry?

2. What's your vision for the next year? What do you think is God's vision for you?

3. Think about some of the people you have turned to for guidance in your family. Are they celebrities or quiet people behind the scenes?

4. How did people in your past make you who you are today?

5. What are some "mountaintop" experiences you had in the past? What made them so special?

6. What lessons from these mountaintop experiences did you learn that you have never forgotten? Who were the people with you? What lessons could you carry into the future?

7. When have you failed at something you thought Jesus and the church trained you to do? How does the disciples' failure help you understand the purpose of that experience of loss?

8. What's your "transfer portal"? How can failure or change help you surrender? What do you need to leave behind?

Chapter 3: Learn from Loss

Summary: Most role models in life are "successful" people with power, money, and influence. Jesus invites us to learn from role models who have endured suffering. The best teacher is Failure itself.

Role Models
The Successful Loser
Professor Failure

Discussion Questions

1. Who are your role models, and what are some of their experiences of loss that you can learn from?

2. What areas of your life are you trying to fix? Is this your assignment or someone else's?

3. Failure can often leave us alone and isolated, but sometimes soul friends are there for us when we least expect it. Their support can be a source of comfort and strength during times of loss or suffering. Who has shown up for you during a time of loss or suffering?

4. When have you suffered an injury or illness and had to wait an extended period of time for healing? What did you learn?

Chapter 4: Failure Class

Summary: Loss is a classroom for disciples. People who appear to be "losers" based on society's standards are role models for believers. When we fail, we are invited to treat the experience like a class in school with Jesus as our teacher.

Six Lessons from the Disciples' Classroom

1. Sit with the loss in Jesus's presence.
2. Ask Jesus to show you your role in the failure.
3. Pray through and name your emotions.
4. Testify to your loss.
5. Grieve the loss of the life you thought was yours.
6. Rise transformed because of the experience.

Discussion Questions

1. Failure is a great teacher, but people rarely want to go through that kind of experience. What failures have you had in the past, and what have you learned from them?

2. This chapter identifies six lessons in Professor Failure's class. Which ones have you tried? Which ones do you need to practice?

3. Transforming negative emotions to others-centered emotions is a powerful part of the process. Pray aloud the prayer of St. Francis of Assisi alone or together with other in a small group.

4. What is the shape of your grief over failure? Has it changed shape over time? Take a moment to draw that picture.

Chapter 5: Think Like a Beginner

Summary: To move toward a life of joy, we need to treat the experience as if we were learning to play an instrument or a sport for the first time. We plan for failure, develop a new virtuous mindset to practice, and track our progress.

Read Philippians 3:1-16; 4:8-9

The Losership Staircase
1. True
2. Honorable
3. Just
4. Holy
5. Pleasurable

6. Reputable
7. Virtuous
8. Praiseworthy

Discussion Questions

1. The loser journey doesn't require expertise, just willingness to think like a toddler exploring. When have you tried to learn something new? What did that feel like?

2. Paul was isolated and in prison when he and Timothy decided to write about the "loser staircase." A place of loneliness can be the beginning of a new mindset. When have you been isolated but sensed God's presence?

3. Take a look at the eight steps on the staircase. Which one is your strongest virtue? Where do you need help?

Chapter 6: The Loser's Circle

Summary: We can't expect to discover joy alone. We need accountability from others and people that we can teach along the way. Develop a group of people and a circular process who can join you on the journey and help you move forward.

Discussion Questions

1. Think about the friends you hang out with the most. Are they service friends, strugglers, or soul friends? Who do you need to spend more time with?

2. Who are your spiritual parents and grandparents? What have they already poured into you? Who could you ask to be a part of this journey with you?

3. Who are the people you could pour into?

4. What areas of your journey would you like to start practicing?

5. Who do you want to learn from?

6. What traditions or teachings have you received?

7. What do you want to read or listen to?

8. What do you want to emulate that you'd like to see in others?

Chapter 7: Characteristics of Joy

Summary: Once we walk through the door, how will we know that we are experiencing a joyful life? As we think virtuously, climbing the stairs with a "losers circle", God's joy fill us in six ways.

God's Kind of Joy

Obedient
Adventurous
Endurance
Listening
Prayerful
Quietly Confident

Discussion Questions

1. Joy is often considered an energetic emotion, but the Bible speaks of several dimensions to joy: a decision, space, promise, and quiet confidence. What kind of joy have you experienced?

2. Read Acts 8:26-40. Listening to Scripture was an essential step that led the eunuch to discover joy. What are some of the steps he took that you could take today?

Chapter 8: Return to Joy

Summary: Joy does not send us backward to relive the past. Joy turns us toward the future that God creates. Our example is the Old Testament character Joseph in Genesis 37-50.

Read Matthew 25:14-30.

Discussion Questions

1. Does Jesus's return evoke fear or excitement for you? How do you react when you hear about the promise of his coming?

2. Instead of planning for the future, Jesus wants us to be prepared for whatever crisis the future brings. What problem in the world are you burdened for? What could God be calling you to respond to?

3. Joseph faced two kinds of injustice and lived long enough to repay his persecutors kindly. What injustice have you faced in your life? Have you been able to be generous or show mercy in these experiences?

Resources for Further Study

Books

Constica Bradatan, *In Praise of Failure: Four Lessons in Humility*, Kindle edition (Cambridge: Harvard University Press, 2023).

Kathleen Brehony, *After the Darkest Hour: How Suffering Begins the Journey to Wisdom* (New York: Henry Holt and Company, 2000).

Arthur Brooks, *From Strength to Strength: Finding Success, Happiness, and Deep Purpose in the Second Half of Life* (New York: Penguin, 2022).

David Brooks, *The Second Mountain: the Quest for a Moral Life* (New York: Random House, 2019).

Amy Edmondson, *Right Kind of Wrong: The Science of Failing Well* (New York: Atria Books), 2023.

Bruce Feiler, *Life Is in the Transitions: Mastering Change at Any Age* (New York: Penguin, 2021).

Barbara Holmes, *Joy Unspeakable: Contemplative Practices of the Black Church*, Second (Minneapolis: Fortress Press, 2017).

Michelle Icard, *Eight Setbacks that Can Make a Child a Success* (New York: Rodale, 2023).

Katrina McGhee, *Taking a Career Break for Dummies* (Hoboken: John Wiley & Sons, 2024).

Jen Marr and Skye Quinn, *Showing Up: a Comprehensive Guide to Comfort and Connection* (New Degree Press, 2022).

Jillian Peterson and James Densley, *The Violence Project: How to Stop a Mass Shooting Epidemic* (Minneapolis: Harry Abrams), 2022.

Daniel Pink, *The Power of Regret: How Looking Back Moves us Forward* (New York: Riverhead, 2022).

April Rinne, *Flux: Eight Superpower for Thriving in Constant Change* (Oakland: Berrett-Koehler, 2021).

Jennifer Breheny Wallace, *Never Enough: When Achievement Culture Becomes Toxic—and What we Can Do About it* (New York: Portfolio/Penguin, 2023).

Matt Watkinson and Csaba Konkoly, *Mastering Uncertainty: How Great Founders, Business Leaders, and Entrepreneurs Thrive in an Unpredictable World* (Dallas: Matt Holt Books, 2023).

Nicholas Thomas Wright, *After You Believe: Why Christian Character Matters* (New York: HarperCollins, 2010), 16.

Prayers

St. Francis of Assisi:

Lord, make me an instrument of your peace:
where there is hatred, let me sow love;
where there is injury, pardon;
where there is doubt, faith;
where there is despair, hope;
where there is darkness, light;
where there is sadness, joy.

O divine Master, grant that I may not so much seek
to be consoled as to console,
to be understood as to understand,
to be loved as to love.
For it is in giving that we receive,
it is in pardoning that we are pardoned,
and it is in dying that we are born to eternal life.
Amen.

Thomas Merton:

My Lord God,
I have no idea where I am going.
I do not see the road ahead of me.
I cannot know for certain where it will end.
nor do I really know myself,
and the fact that I think I am following your will
does not mean that I am actually doing so.
But I believe that the desire to please you
does in fact please you.
And I hope I have that desire in all that I am doing.

I hope that I will never do anything apart from that desire.
And I know that if I do this you will lead me by the right road,
though I may know nothing about it.
Therefore will I trust you always though
I may seem to be lost and in the shadow of death.
I will not fear, for you are ever with me,
and you will never leave me to face my perils alone.

Chapter in *Leading Lives that Matter*, edited by Mark R. Schwehn and Dorothy Bass (Grand Rapids: Eerdmans), 450.

Images

The Losership Staircase

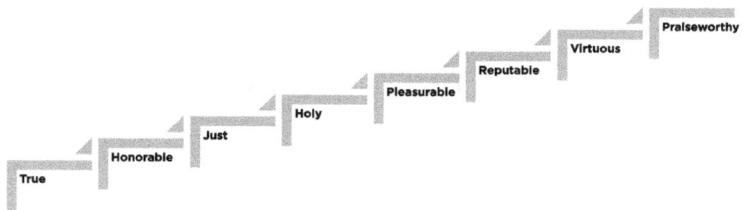

The Losership Cycle

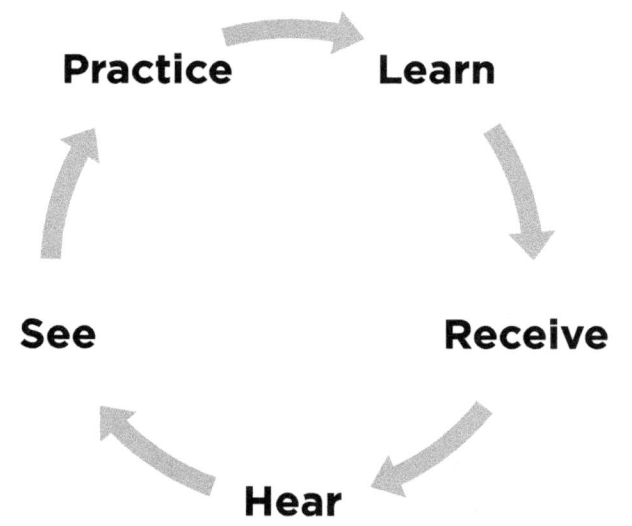

Worksheet 1: Joyful Life Journal and Tracker

Choose a loss in your life that is still teaching you in some way. Answer these questions as you reflect on the loss.

1. Sit with the loss in Jesus's presence. What did Jesus say to you?

2. Ask Jesus to show you your role in the failure. What did you admit or learn?

3. Pray through and name your emotions. Write them down.

4. Testify to your loss. Who have you told about it, and what did they say?

5. Grieve the loss of the life you thought was yours. Try to draw the shape of your grief.

6. Rise transformed because of the experience. What did you leave behind? In what ways are you transformed?

Worksheet 2: Your Loser's Circle

My spiritual parents or grandparents who pour wisdom, love, and care into me:

The people I want to pour my wisdom, love, and care into:

What I want to "practice" with my loser's circle:

Worksheet 3: Tracking Your Mindset

1. Begin each day pondering the Loser's Staircase (see p. 61). What do you expect to see and do that is…

True
Honorable
Just
Holy
Pleasurable
Reputable
Virtuous
Praiseworthy

2. End each day the same way, but this time consider how often you saw or thought something that was…

True
Honorable
Just
Holy
Pleasurable
Reputable
Virtuous
Praiseworthy

3. Each week, use this tracker chart to reflect on what you experienced or did that reflected the eight virtues.

What habits and thoughts did I have about the following virtues?

Virtue	Week 1	Week 2	Week 3	Week 4	Week 5	Week 6
True						
Honorable						
Just						
Holy						
Pleasurable						
Reputable						
Virtuous						
Praiseworthy						

4. Each week, track a different practice you want to try as you work with your loser's circle. Who do you want to learn from, what tradition or teaching have you received, what do you want to hear/read, what do you see in others you want to emulate, and what can you put into practice?

Practices	Week 1	Week 2	Week 3	Week 4	Week 5	Week 6
Learn						
Receive						
Hear/Read						
See						
Practice						

5. At the end of each month, reflect on your experiences. Where have you seen yourself become increasingly…

Obedient
Adventurous
Enduring
Attentive
Prayerful
Quietly Confident

Notes

Preface

1. Bruce Feiler, *Life Is in the Transitions: Mastering Change at Any Age* (New York: Penguin, 2021), 231.
2. *Our Epidemic of Loneliness and Isolation: The U.S. Surgeon General's Advisory on the Healing Effects of Social Connection and Community*, Washington DC, 2023, https://www.hhs.gov/sites/default/files/surgeon-general-social-connection-advisory.pdf, p. 4.
3. Jillian Peterson and James Densley, *The Violence Project: How to Stop a Mass Shooting Epidemic* (Minneapolis: Harry Abrams, 2022), 25.

Chapter 1

1. Scholars call this idea "Deuteronomic theology."
2. See Arthur Brooks, *From Strength to Strength: Finding Success, Happiness, and Deep Purpose in the Second Half of Life* (New York: Penguin, 2022), 74. Also see Luke 12:15.
3. Brené Brown explores this idea in *Dare to Lead: Brave Work, Tough Conversations, Whole Hearts* (New York: Random House, 2018), 247.
4. Costica Bradatan, *In Praise of Failure: Four Lessons in Humility*, Kindle edition (Cambridge: Harvard University Press, 2023), 120.

Chapter 2

1. William D. Shiell, *Sessions with Matthew: Becoming a Family of Faith* (Macon, GA: Smyth and Helwys, 2008), 6.
2. Jason M. Zurawki, *Jewish Paideia: Education and Identity in the Hellenistic Diaspora* (Minneapolis: Fortress Press, 2023), 178.

3. Unless otherwise noted, all Scripture is taken from the *New Revised Standard Version Bible: Anglicized Edition*, copyright © 1989, 1995 National Council of the Churches of Christ in the United States of America. Used by permission. All rights reserved worldwide. http://nrsvbibles.org.

Chapter 3

1. The verb in Greek in the Septuagint book of Esther is the same as the one in Mark 9.

Chapter 4

1. Dietrich Bonhoeffer, *The Cost of Discipleship*, revised and unabridged (New York: Collier Books, 1963), 99.

2. Bonhoeffer, *Cost of Discipleship*, s101.

3. James W. Pennebaker and John Evans, *Expressive Writing: Words that Heal* (Bedford, IN: Idyll Arbor, 2014).

4. Brown, *Dare to Lead*, 267.

5. Brown, *Dare to Lead*, 247.

6. Brooks, *Strength to Strength*, 179–80.

7. Bradatan, *In Praise of Failure*, 235.

8. William Blevins, "It's Hard to Say Goodbye: Grief from a Pastoral Care Perspective," in *Assaulted by Grief: Finding God in the Broken Places*, ed. David Crutchley and Gerald Borchert (Jefferson City, TN: Moss Creek Press, 2011), 135–36.

9. Kathleen Brehony, *After the Darkest Hour: How Suffering Begins the Journey to Wisdom* (New York: Henry Holt and Company, 2000), 106.

Chapter 5

1. Amy Edmondson, *Right Kind of Wrong: The Science of Failing Well* (New York: Atria Books, 2023), 39.

2. Cicero *Tusc. Disp.* 3.16.35-3.17.37.

3. See Ben Witherington III, *Paul's Letter to the Philippians: A Socio-Rhetorical Commentary* (Grand Rapids, MI: Eerdmans, 2011), 256.

4. Aristotle noted that the qualities in a stair-step function as parts or subdivisions of virtue and are the most useful for practicing virtue in the community (Aristotle, *Rhetoric* 1.9.5).

5. See Witherington, *Paul's Letter to the Philippians*, 256.

NOTES

6. Seneca suggests something similar to a mother named Marcia as she deals with her grief over the loss of her son. Seneca urges a certain kind of reflection and thinking that will address her grief (Seneca *Ad Marc.* 24.1-10). See Paul Holloway, *Philippians: A Commentary*, Hermeneia (Minneapolis: Fortress Press, 2017), 184.

7. See John Reumann, *Philippians: A New Translation with Introduction and Commentary*, vol. 33b, Anchor Yale Bible (New Haven: Yale University Press, 2008), 617.

8. Reumann, *Philippians*, 617.

9. See Dio Chrysostom, *Orationes/Discourses* 3.97.

10. See Plato, *Gorgias* 507e; 513a; Polybius, *Histories* 10.5; Sophocles, *Phil.* 585; Cassius Dio, *Roman Histories* 9.1; Eusebius, *Ecclesiastical Histories* 7.16.

11. See Gerald F. Hawthorne, *Philippians*, Word Biblical Commentary 43 (Waco: Word Books, 1983), 188; Pleasure in Music and its effect on character Aristotle, *Politics* 8.1340a; Jacob beloved by his mother Rebeka (Josephus, *A.J.* 1.258) on the importance of friendship over military power and the delight/pleasure of a symposium or sacrificing to the gods with friends and people who like you pleasure it provides (Dio Chrysostom, *Orationes/ Discourses* 3.97) Endearing oneself to people and the gods because you're able to tame your desires (Plato *Gorgias* 507e; also winning their affection 513a); obtaining favor (Polybius *Histories* 10.5) Kindly disposed toward someone to reveal battle plans. (Sophocles *Phil.* 585) to be viewed favorable (Cassius Dio *Roman Histories* 9.1; Eusebius *Ecclesiastical Histories* 7.16).

12. See Reumann, *Philippians*, 618.

13. See Polybius, *Histories* 31.3.4; Aeschylus, *Suppliant Women* 490.

14. For a longer discussion of the relationship between Aristotle's concept of virtue and Paul's, see Nicholas Thomas Wright, *After You Believe: Why Christian Character Matters* (New York: HarperCollins, 2010), 16, and Julien C. H. Smith, *Paul and the Good Life: Transformation and Citizenship in the Commonwealth of God* (Waco: Baylor University Press, 2020), 5–7. The idea of "virtue ethics" is beyond the scope of this commentary. However, I suggest that Paul adapts the idea of virtue from the Greeks and Romans to his rhetorical purposes. Namely, he wants to set up a new system of virtues to which the colonists can aspire and the Philippian community will admire. The appeal is emotional rather than conceptual and results in reconciling those who are at odds, giving confidence to the listeners, and setting up a process going forward that they can continue to apply in their context.

Chapter 6

1. See Lidija Novakovic, *Philippians: A Handbook on the Greek Text*, Baylor Handbook on the Greek New Testament (Waco: Baylor University Press, 2020), 113.
2. See Witherington, *Paul's Letter to the Philippians*, 258.
3. For more, see William D. Shiell, *Delivering from Memory: The Effect of Performance on the Early Christian Audience* (Eugene, OR: Pickwick Publications, 2011), 67.
4. See Demosthenes's speech in Plutarch, *Lives of the Ten Orators* 9.850e, where the second part is the received tradition that was passed on.
5. William D Shiell, *Reading Acts: The Lector and the Early Christian Audience*, Biblical Interpretation Series 70 (Leiden: Brill Academic Publishers, 2004), 107.
6. Dirk Schenkeveld, "Prose Usages of Akouein to Read," *Classical Quarterly* 42 (1992): 133.
7. The word *akouein* and the Greek word for read, *anagignwskei*, were often used together and interchangeably, indicating the importance of understanding and listening to what was read (Plutarch, *On Reading the Poets*; Quintilian, *Inst.* 10.1.10). In this context, the reading aloud of Paul and Timothy's epistle was as significant as listening to what Paul said in person.
8. Plutarch, *Rect. rat. aud.* 5; *Mor.* 38E; Seneca, *Ep.* 3.2.25.3-3.2.35.4. In 4 Maccabees, the martyred mother and sons are role models. They already yielded a harvest of righteousness to the glory and praise of God (4 Macc 1:11). Now their virtues will continue to be lauded and inspire others (17:12-23).
9. George Vaillant, *Spiritual Evolution: A Scientific Defense of Faith* (New York: Broadway Books, 2008), 67.
10. Edmondson, *Failing Well*, 48.
11. Parker Palmer, *A Hidden Wholeness: The Journey Toward an Undivided Life* (San Francisco: Jossey-Bass, 2004), 61.

Chapter 7

1. Barbara Holmes, *Joy Unspeakable: Contemplative Practices of the Black Church* (Minneapolis: Fortress Press, 2017), 98–99.
2. Brooks, *Strength to Strength*, 121.
3. Holmes, *Joy Unspeakable*, 82.

NOTES

Chapter 8

1. A. J. Conyers, *The End: What Jesus Really Said about the Last Things* (Downers Grove, IL: InterVarsity Press, 1995), 114.
2. Richard A. Rohr, *Falling Upward: A Spirituality for the Two Halves of Life* (San Francisco: Josey-Bass, 2011), 58.
3. Jürgen Moltmann, *Theology and Joy* (London: SCM Press, 1973), 63.
4. Moltmann, *Theology and Joy*, 63.
5. Rebecca Solnit, *A Paradise Built in Hell: The Extraordinary Communities That Arise in Disaster* (New York: Penguin, 2009), 297.

www.ingramcontent.com/pod-product-compliance
Lightning Source LLC
LaVergne TN
LVHW051133080426
835510LV00018B/2396